Hands-On Standards®, Common Core Edition

Grade 2

ETA hand2mind
hands-on learning
for growing minds

Hands-On Standards®, Common Core Edition
Grade 2

hand2mind 78866

ISBN 978-0-7406-9431-8

Vernon Hills, IL 60061-1862
800-445-5985
www.hand2mind.com

Printed in the United States of America.

12 13 14 15 16 17 18 19 20 21   10 9 8 7 6 5 4 3 2

Contents

Blackline Masters

Introduction

How do we help children find meaning in mathematics? That is, how do we give children more than a rote script for reciting facts and churning out computations? How do we help children develop understanding?

Hands-On Standards®, Common Core Edition Grade 2 is an easy-to-use reference manual for teachers who want to help children discover meaning in mathematics. Each of the manual's 29 lessons demonstrates a hands-on exploration using manipulatives. The goal is to help children get a physical sense of a problem—to help children get their hands on the concepts they need to know and to help them "see" the meaning.

Each lesson in *Hands-On Standards* targets a clearly stated objective. The main part of a lesson offers a story problem that children can relate to and has the children work on the problem using a hands-on approach. Full-color photographs demonstrate the suggested steps. In addition to the main activity, each lesson includes suggested points of discussion, ideas for more exploration, a formative assessment item, and practice pages to help children solidify their understanding. The instructional model is a progression from concrete to abstract.

This book is divided into four sections—Operations and Algebraic Thinking, Number and Operations in Base Ten, Measurement and Data, and Geometry. These correspond to the four content domains for Grade 2 as cited in the *Common Core State Standards for Mathematics*.

Each lesson in this book uses one or more of the following manipulatives:

Base Ten Blocks • **2-cm Color Cubes** • **Coin Tiles** • **Color Tiles** • **Cuisenaire® Rods** • **Geoboards** • **Geared Mini-Clock** • **Inchworms™** • **Inchworms™ Ruler** • **Two-Color Counters**

Read on to find out how *Hands-On Standards, Common Core Edition Grade 2* can help the children in your class find meaning in math and build a foundation for future math success!

1

A Walk Through a Lesson

Each lesson in *Hands-On Standards* includes many features, including background information, objectives, pacing and grouping suggestions, discussion questions, and ideas for further activities, all in addition to the step-by-step, hands-on activity instruction. Take a walk through a lesson to see an explanation of each feature.

Lesson Introduction
A brief introduction explores the background of the concepts and skills covered in each lesson. It shows how they fit into the larger context of children's mathematical development.

Try It! Arrow
In order to provide a transition from the introduction to the activity, an arrow draws attention to the Try It! activity on the next page. When the activity has been completed, return to the first page to complete the lesson.

Objective
The **Objective** summarizes the skill or concept children will learn through the hands-on lesson.

Common Core State Standards
Each lesson has been created to align with one or more of the **Common Core State Standards for Mathematics**.

Talk About It
The **Talk About It** section provides post-activity discussion topics and questions. Discussion reinforces activity concepts and provides the opportunity to make sure children have learned and understood the concepts and skills.

Solve It
Solve It gives students a chance to show what they've learned. Children are asked to return to and solve the original word problem. They might summarize the lesson concept through drawing or writing, or extend the skill through a new variation on the problem.

More Ideas
More Ideas provides additional activities and suggestions for teaching about the lesson concept using a variety of manipulatives. These ideas might be suggestions for additional practice with the skill or an extension of the lesson.

Formative Assessment
Formative assessments allow for on-going feedback on children's understanding of the concept.

LESSON 3

Objective
Identify even and odd number patterns.

Common Core State Standards
- **2.OA.3** Determine whether a group of objects (up to 20) has an odd or even number of members, e.g., by pairing objects or counting them by 2s; write an equation to express an even number as a sum of two equal addends.

Operations and Algebraic Thinking
Even and Odd Number Patterns

Children at this stage have learned to identify some attributes of numbers—such as whether they are greater or less than another number—as well as attributes of geometric shapes. Here, children learn to identify a new attribute of a number: whether it is *odd* or *even*. Learning to recognize odd and even number patterns prepares children for later development of more complex algebraic and geometric concepts.

Try It! Perform the Try It! activity on the next page.

Talk About It
Discuss the Try It! activity.
- Have children look at their completed Hundred Charts (BLM 2). **Ask:** *Which numbers from 1 to 10 are odd numbers? Which are even numbers?*
- **Say:** *Look at the even numbers on the Hundred Chart.* **Ask:** *Which digits are in the ones place?* **Say:** *Now look at the odd numbers.* **Ask:** *Which digits are in the ones place?*
- **Ask:** *If a two- or three-digit number has a 0, 2, 4, 6, or an 8 in the ones place, is the number even or odd? If a two- or three-digit number has a 1, 3, 5, 7, or 9 in the ones place, is the number even or odd? What pattern can you see?*

Solve It
With children, reread the problem. **Ask:** *How can Jody find out if everyone in her class will have a buddy?* Ask children to write letters to Jody telling her about even and odd numbers and how she can use what she learns about them to find her answer.

More Ideas
For other ways to teach about even and odd number patterns—
- Have one child pull a handful of Snap Cubes® from a bag. Another child puts the cubes in pairs. Together they determine if the number of cubes is odd or even.
- Distribute copies of Ten Frames (BLM 3) to children. Have children use Two-Color Counters to model numbers in the ten frames. Explain that if a number is even, every counter will have a partner in its row. If a number is odd, there will be one counter without a partner in its row.

Formative Assessment
Have children try the following problem.

Place the following numbers in the sorting circles: 6, 9, 23, 38, 72, 97.

16

2

Try It!

The **Try It!** activity opens with **Pacing** and **Grouping** guides. The **Pacing** guide indicates about how much time it will take for children to complete the activity, including the post-activity discussion. The **Grouping** guide recommends whether children should work independently, in pairs, or in small groups.

Next, the **Try It!** activity is introduced with a real-world story problem. Children will "solve" the problem by performing the hands-on activity. The word problem provides a context for the hands-on work and the lesson skill.

The **Materials** box lists the type and quantity of materials that children will use to complete the activity, including manipulatives such as Color Tiles and Base Ten Blocks.

This section of the page also includes any instruction that children may benefit from before starting the activity, such as a review of foundational mathematical concepts or an introduction to new ones.

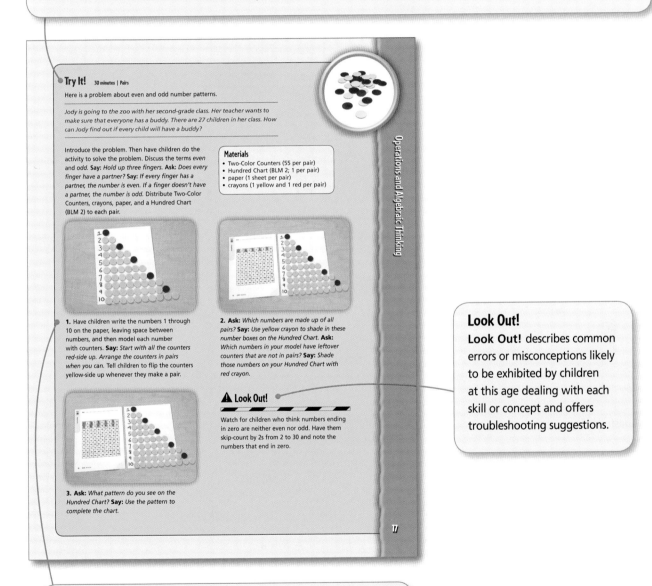

Try It! 30 minutes | Pairs

Here is a problem about even and odd number patterns.

Jody is going to the zoo with her second-grade class. Her teacher wants to make sure that everyone has a buddy. There are 27 children in her class. How can Jody find out if every child will have a buddy?

Introduce the problem. Then have children do the activity to solve the problem. Discuss the terms *even* and *odd.* **Say:** *Hold up three fingers.* **Ask:** *Does every finger have a partner?* **Say:** *If every finger has a partner, the number is even. If a finger doesn't have a partner, the number is odd.* Distribute Two-Color Counters, crayons, paper, and a Hundred Chart (BLM 2) to each pair.

Materials
• Two-Color Counters (55 per pair)
• Hundred Chart (BLM 2; 1 per pair)
• paper (1 sheet per pair)
• crayons (1 yellow and 1 red per pair)

1. Have children write the numbers 1 through 10 on the paper, leaving space between numbers, and then model each number with counters. **Say:** *Start with all the counters red-side up. Arrange the counters in pairs when you can.* Tell children to flip the counters yellow-side up whenever they make a pair.

2. Ask: *Which numbers are made up of all pairs?* **Say:** *Use yellow crayon to shade in these number boxes on the Hundred Chart.* **Ask:** *Which numbers in your model have leftover counters that are not in pairs?* **Say:** *Shade those numbers on your Hundred Chart with red crayon.*

⚠ Look Out!

Watch for children who think numbers ending in zero are neither even nor odd. Have them skip-count by 2s from 2 to 30 and note the numbers that end in zero.

3. Ask: *What pattern do you see on the Hundred Chart?* **Say:** *Use the pattern to complete the chart.*

Operations and Algebraic Thinking

17

Look Out!

Look Out! describes common errors or misconceptions likely to be exhibited by children at this age dealing with each skill or concept and offers troubleshooting suggestions.

Step-by-Step Activity Procedure

The hands-on activity itself is the core of each lesson. It is presented in three—or sometimes four—steps, each of which includes instruction in how children should use manipulatives and other materials to address the introductory word problem and master the lesson's skill or concept. An accompanying photograph illustrates each step.

A Walk Through a Student Page

Each lesson is followed by a corresponding set of student pages. These pages take the child from the concrete to the abstract, completing the instructional cycle. Children begin by using manipulatives, move to creating visual representations, and then complete the cycle by working with abstract mathematical symbols.

Exercise
Concrete and **Representational** exercises (pictorial representations of the featured manipulative) help children bridge conceptual learning to symbolic mathematics.

Standards-Based Math Practice
Abstract exercises provide standards-based math practice to allow children to deepen their understanding of the featured skill.

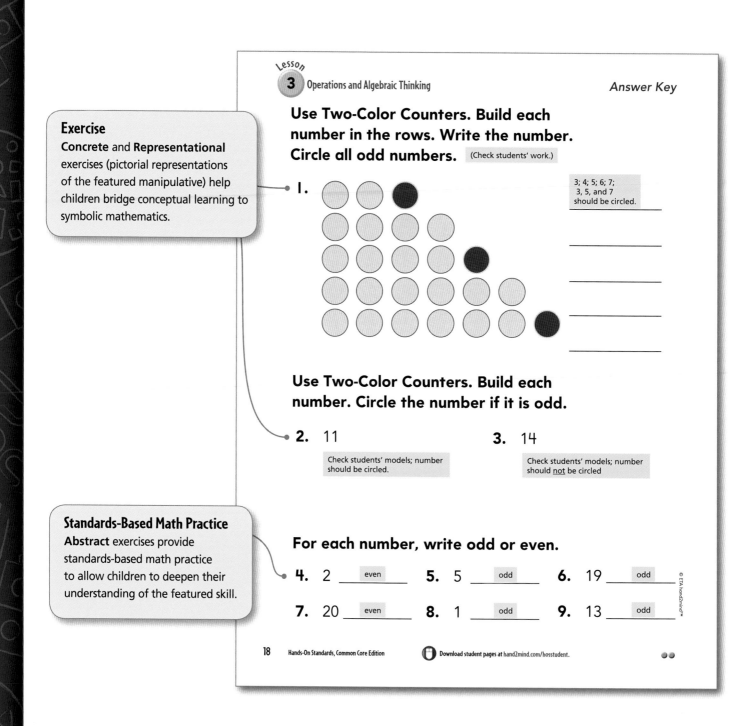

Lesson 3 · Operations and Algebraic Thinking

Answer Key

Use Two-Color Counters. Build each number in the rows. Write the number. Circle all odd numbers. (Check students' work.)

1.

3; 4; 5; 6; 7;
3, 5, and 7
should be circled.

Use Two-Color Counters. Build each number. Circle the number if it is odd.

2. 11
Check students' models; number should be circled.

3. 14
Check students' models; number should not be circled

For each number, write odd or even.

4. 2 ___even___   5. 5 ___odd___   6. 19 ___odd___

7. 20 ___even___   8. 1 ___odd___   9. 13 ___odd___

18 Hands-On Standards, Common Core Edition   Download student pages at hand2mind.com/hosstudent.

© ETA hand2mind™

4

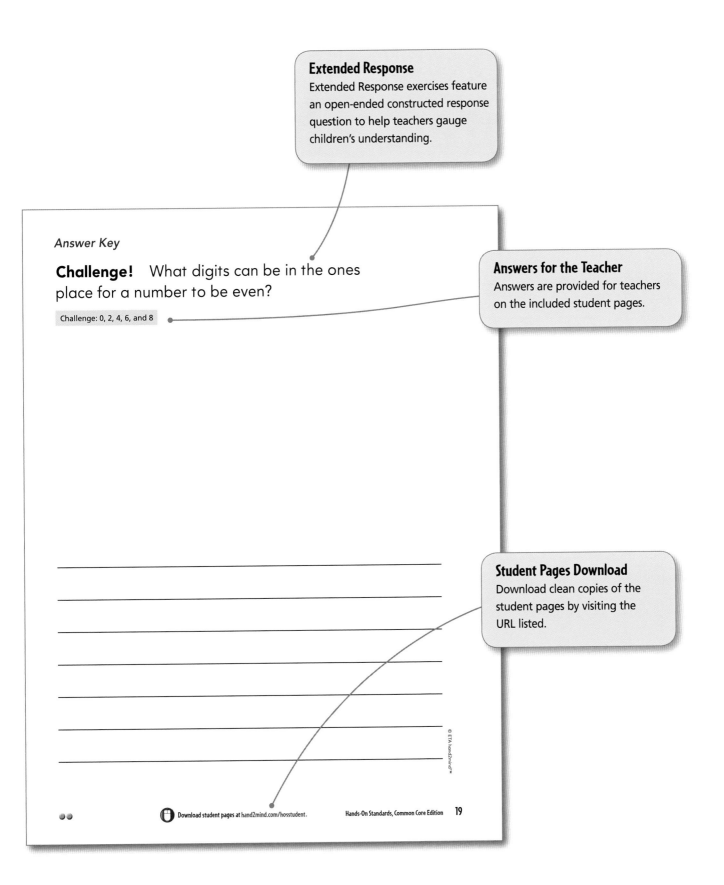

Extended Response
Extended Response exercises feature an open-ended constructed response question to help teachers gauge children's understanding.

Answer Key

Challenge! What digits can be in the ones place for a number to be even?

Challenge: 0, 2, 4, 6, and 8

Answers for the Teacher
Answers are provided for teachers on the included student pages.

Student Pages Download
Download clean copies of the student pages by visiting the URL listed.

© ETA hand2mind™

Hands-On Standards, Common Core Edition   19

Operations and Algebraic Thinking

In second grade, children continue their work with addition and subtraction. They work on word problems within 100 by representing and solving three types of one- and two-step word problems—*result* unknown, *change* unknown, and *start* unknown.

Children internalize addition and subtraction facts within 20 and develop fluency by repeatedly using strategies that make sense to them. They move beyond counting and counting-on to methods such as make a ten, "doubles," and "near doubles." They are called to know from memory all sums of two one-digit numbers. The goal is to give children many experiences using manipulatives and visual representations, not to simply present a list of facts for them to memorize.

Second graders use their knowledge of "doubles" to understand the concepts of *odd* and *even*. They learn that if a number can be broken into two equal addends, then the number is even. They determine whether a group of objects has an odd or even number of members by using strategies such as pairing objects, counting by 2's, and writing an equation. Children also use arrays to work with repeated addition, a foundational concept necessary for learning multiplication.

The Grade 2 Common Core State Standards for Operations and Algebraic Thinking specify that children should—

- Represent and solve problems involving addition and subtraction.
- Add and subtract within 20.
- Work with equal groups of objects to gain foundations for multiplication.

The following hands-on activities help children internalize addition and subtraction facts and solve one- and two-step problems. Mathematically proficient second graders develop a foundation for applying problem-solving strategies and become independently proficient at using those strategies to solve new tasks. They are expected to persevere while solving tasks when "stuck" by re-examining the task in different ways, figuring what they know and don't know, and continuing to solve it.

Operations and Algebraic Thinking

Contents

Common Core State Standards

- **2.OA.1** Use addition and subtraction within 100 to solve one- and two-step word problems involving situations of adding to, taking from, putting together, taking apart, and comparing, with unknowns in all positions, e.g., by using drawings and equations with a symbol for the unknown number to represent the problem.

Operations and Algebraic Thinking

Addition and Subtraction

As children become fluent in computation, they begin to apply their understanding of operations to problem-solving situations. Children address equations that have an unknown number and learn to work backward by using the inverse operation to solve for the missing number. In this lesson, children model addition and subtraction number sentences and experience firsthand how the two operations are related.

Try It! *Perform the Try It! activity on the next page.*

Talk About It

Discuss the Try It! activity.

- **Ask:** *How do you use subtraction to find a missing addend, or adding number? How do you use addition to solve a subtraction problem?*

- **Ask:** *How can I use subtraction to find out what number plus 13 equals 29?* Write _____ + 13 = 29 on the board. Children should explain that they would subtract 13 from 29. Write 29 – 13 = _____ on the board. Invite children to solve.

- **Ask:** *How can I use addition to show what number minus 23 equals 15?* Write _____ – 23 = 15 on the board. Children should explain that they would add 23 to 15 to find the answer. Write 15 + 23 = _____ on the board. Invite children to solve.

Solve It

With children, reread the problem. Have children explain in writing how they solved the problem. Then have children show the solution using both an addition and a subtraction sentence.

More Ideas

For other ways to teach about addition and subtraction number sentences—

- Invite children to solve additional problems using Base Ten Blocks and the Missing Numbers Worksheet (BLM 1). Have children record their completed addition and subtraction sentences for each problem.

- Have children write their own addition and subtraction problems involving families of bears. Have children exchange problems with a partner. Then partners use the inverse operation and Three Bear Family® Counters to model and solve the problems.

Formative Assessment

Have children try the following problem.

Circle the addition sentence that solves this problem: _____ – 11 = 16

A. 11 + 5 = 16   **B.** 16 + 11 = 27   **C.** 5 + 6 = 11   **D.** 11 + 11 = 22

Try It! 25 minutes | Groups of 4

Here is a problem about addition and subtraction number sentences.

Of the 18 students in our class, 7 students have perfect attendance so far this year. How many students do not have perfect attendance?

Introduce the problem. Then have children do the activity to solve the problem. Distribute Cuisenaire Rods, worksheets, and pencils to children. Remind children that white rods have a value of 1, orange rods have a value of 10, and other colors have values in between.

Materials

- Cuisenaire® Rods (half a set per group)
- Missing Numbers Worksheet (BLM 1; 1 per group)
- pencils (1 per group)

1. Say: *Look at the Missing Numbers Worksheet. We will use it to find what number you add to 7 to get 18.* Have children use rods to model the addition problem on the worksheet.

2. Ask: *How can we solve this addition sentence?* Guide children to see that they should subtract to find the missing number. Have children complete the train on the second line to match the first train.

⚠ Look Out!

Watch out for children who seem to start over from scratch when forming a subtraction problem to solve for a missing addend in an addition problem. Point out that the numbers in both problems should be identical; only their positions and the operation change. Demonstrate by showing how rods placed on the Missing Numbers Worksheet change places.

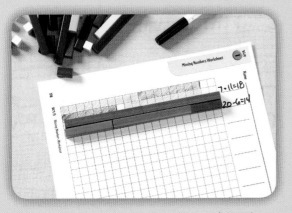

3. Have children use rods to solve a subtraction problem. Write *20 – _____ = 14* on the board. **Ask:** *How can we solve this subtraction sentence?* Have children model the problem on their worksheet and use addition to solve it.

Use Cuisenaire Rods to build each model. Write each missing number. (Check students' work.)

1.

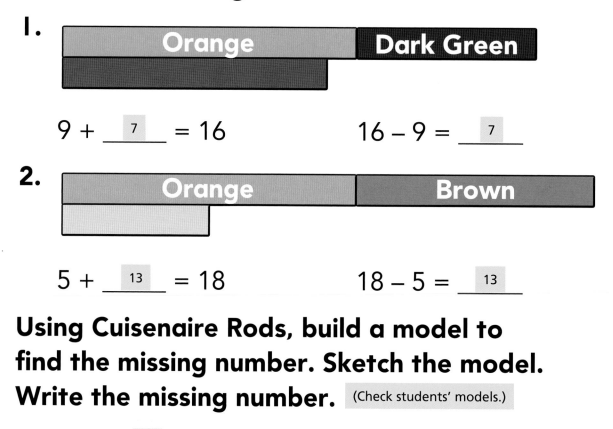

$9 +$ _7_ $= 16$ $16 - 9 =$ _7_

2.

$5 +$ _13_ $= 18$ $18 - 5 =$ _13_

Using Cuisenaire Rods, build a model to find the missing number. Sketch the model. Write the missing number. (Check students' models.)

3. $5 +$ _12_ $= 17$ **4.** $17 -$ _12_ $= 5$

Find the missing number in each addition or subtraction sentence.

5. $7 +$ _8_ $= 15$ **6.** $12 +$ _11_ $= 23$

7. $22 -$ _17_ $= 5$ **8.** $3 +$ _15_ $= 18$

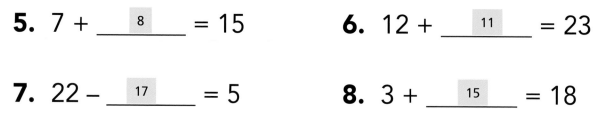

© ETA hand2mind™

Challenge! Use the model in Question 2 to describe two different ways to find the missing number.

Challenge: (Sample) You can count the number of white rods it takes to make the second train the same length as the first. You can use the lengths of any other combination of rods (e.g., 10 + 3) that you use to make the second train the same length as the first.

_____

_____

_____

_____

_____

_____

Objective

Write and solve number sentences from problem situations that express relationships involving addition and subtraction.

Common Core State Standards

- **2.OA.1** Use addition and subtraction within 100 to solve one- and two-step word problems involving situations of adding to, taking from, putting together, taking apart, and comparing, with unknowns in all positions, e.g., by using drawings and equations with a symbol for the unknown number to represent the problem.
- **2.NBT.7** Add and subtract within 1000, using concrete models or drawings and strategies based on place value, properties of operations, and/ or the relationship between addition and subtraction; relate the strategy to a written method. Understand that in adding or subtracting three-digit numbers, one adds or subtracts hundreds and hundreds, tens and tens, ones and ones; and sometimes it is necessary to compose or decompose tens or hundreds.

Operations and Algebraic Thinking

Writing Number Sentences

A number sentence is an expression that contains numbers; symbols of operations; and a greater than, less than, or equal sign. Number sentences are used as a way to record the computation process of solving a mathematical problem. In order to write a number sentence from a problem situation, the numbers involved, as well as the relationship between them, must be identified.

Try It! Perform the Try It! activity on the next page.

Talk About It

Discuss the Try It! activity.

- Have children look at the Base Ten Blocks they used in the activity.
- **Ask:** *How did you show the number of cookies Danielle baked? What blocks did you use? Why? How did you show the cookies she sold? How can you take away the cookies Danielle sold?*
- **Ask:** *What number sentence did you write to show your solution to the problem? How do you know that is correct? How can you take away the cookies Danielle sold?*

Solve It

With children, reread the problem. Ask children to draw pictures of Danielle's cookies or symbols to represent them. Have children mark the cookies sold in some way. Then, have them label the picture with the number sentence and write a sentence explaining how they know the number sentence is correct.

More Ideas

For other ways to teach about writing number sentences—

- Have children use Snap Cubes® to act out a problem situation and write the corresponding number sentence as the situation is acted out.
- Have children use a Hundred Chart (BLM 2) to represent a problem situation and label the chart with the corresponding number sentence.
- Have children use Ten Frames (BLM 3) to represent the problem. Have them complete one ten frame and partially fill another to represent the cookies. Ask children how they might use the make-a-ten strategy to subtract.

Formative Assessment

Have children try the following problem.

Draw pictures to help solve this problem, and write a number sentence to show your work. Matt has cucumbers in his garden. Yesterday he picked 7, and today he picked 8. How many cucumbers did Matt pick altogether?

Try It! 30 minutes | Independent

Here is a problem about writing number sentences.

Danielle baked 18 chocolate chip cookies for a bake sale. She sold 9 cookies. How many cookies did she have left?

Introduce the problem. Then have children do the activity to solve the problem.

Distribute Base Ten Blocks, paper, and pencils to children.

Materials
- Base Ten Blocks (rods and units)
- paper (1 sheet per child)
- pencils (1 per child)

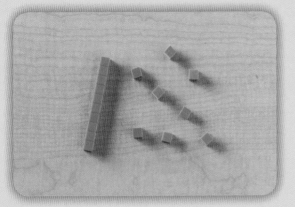

1. To begin, have children choose Base Ten Blocks to show the number of cookies Danielle baked. Show how many cookies were sold.

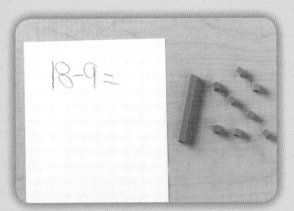

2. Have children write a number sentence on a sheet of paper that can be used to find the number of cookies that were left.

3. Ask: *Do you have to combine two numbers or take a number away from another to find the answer? How can you take away 9 cookies? Do you have to exchange any of the blocks? How many cookies were left?*

⚠ Look Out!

Watch for children who confuse the operations, either in calculation or in representation with a symbol. Remind children to first decide if they need to combine or take away to find the answer. Prompt them to write the corresponding sequence of numbers and symbols. You also can have children make 9 jumps backward on a naked number line to show the taking away.

Use Base Ten Blocks. Write a number sentence for the model. (Check students' work.)

1.

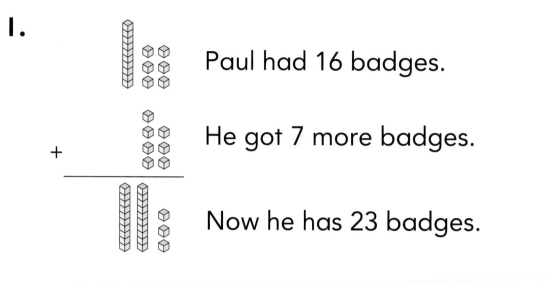

Paul had 16 badges.

He got 7 more badges.

Now he has 23 badges.

Number sentence: _____16 + 7 = 23_____

Use Base Ten Blocks. Model the problem. Draw the model. Write a number sentence to solve.

2. Sally had 16 blocks. She gave away 9 of them. How many does she have now?

Number sentence: _____16 − 9 = 7_____

Write a number sentence to solve.

3. I had 7 coins. I got 8 more coins. How many coins do I have now?

Number sentence: _____7 + 8 = 15_____

 Download student pages at hand2mind.com/hosstudent.

© ETA hand2mind™

Challenge! What symbols do you use to write a number sentence for addition? What symbols do you use to write a number sentence for subtraction?

Challenge: + and =; – and =

_____

_____

_____

_____

_____

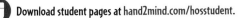
© ETA hand2mind™

Objective

Identify even and odd number patterns.

Common Core State Standards

- **2.OA.3** Determine whether a group of objects (up to 20) has an odd or even number of members, e.g., by pairing objects or counting them by 2s; write an equation to express an even number as a sum of two equal addends.

Operations and Algebraic Thinking

Even and Odd Number Patterns

Children at this stage have learned to identify some attributes of numbers—such as whether they are greater or less than another number—as well as attributes of geometric shapes. Here, children learn to identify a new attribute of a number: whether it is *odd* or *even*. Learning to recognize odd and even number patterns prepares children for later development of more complex algebraic and geometric concepts.

Try It! *Perform the Try It! activity on the next page.*

Talk About It

Discuss the Try It! activity.

- Have children look at their completed Hundred Charts (BLM 2). **Ask:** *Which numbers from 1 to 10 are odd numbers? Which are even numbers?*

- **Say:** *Look at the even numbers on the Hundred Chart.* **Ask:** *Which digits are in the ones place?* **Say:** *Now look at the odd numbers.* **Ask:** *Which digits are in the ones place?*

- **Ask:** *If a two- or three-digit number has a 0, 2, 4, 6, or an 8 in the ones place, is the number even or odd? If a two- or three-digit number has a 1, 3, 5, 7, or 9 in the ones place, is the number even or odd? What pattern can you see?*

Solve It

With children, reread the problem. **Ask:** *How can Jody find out if everyone in her class will have a buddy?* Ask children to write letters to Jody telling her about even and odd numbers and how she can use what she learns about them to find her answer.

More Ideas

For other ways to teach about even and odd number patterns—

- Have one child pull a handful of Snap Cubes® from a bag. Another child puts the cubes in pairs. Together they determine if the number of cubes is odd or even.

- Distribute copies of Ten Frames (BLM 3) to children. Have children use Two-Color Counters to model numbers in the ten frames. Explain that if a number is even, every counter will have a partner in its row. If a number is odd, there will be one counter without a partner in its row.

Formative Assessment

Have children try the following problem.

Place the following numbers in the sorting circles: 6, 9, 23, 38, 72, 97.

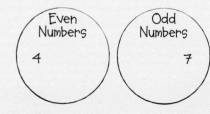

Try It! 30 minutes | Pairs

Here is a problem about even and odd number patterns.

Jody is going to the zoo with her second-grade class. Her teacher wants to make sure that everyone has a buddy. There are 27 children in her class. How can Jody find out if every child will have a buddy?

Introduce the problem. Then have children do the activity to solve the problem. Discuss the terms *even* and *odd.* **Say:** *Hold up three fingers.* **Ask:** *Does every finger have a partner?* **Say:** *If every finger has a partner, the number is even. If a finger doesn't have a partner, the number is odd.* Distribute Two-Color Counters, crayons, paper, and a Hundred Chart (BLM 2) to each pair.

Materials

- Two-Color Counters (55 per pair)
- Hundred Chart (BLM 2; 1 per pair)
- paper (1 sheet per pair)
- crayons (1 yellow and 1 red per pair)

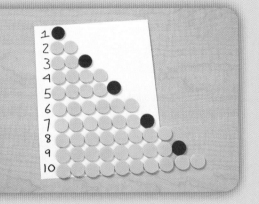

1. Have children write the numbers 1 through 10 on the paper, leaving space between numbers, and then model each number with counters. **Say:** *Start with all the counters red-side up. Arrange the counters in pairs when you can. Tell children to flip the counters yellow-side up whenever they make a pair.*

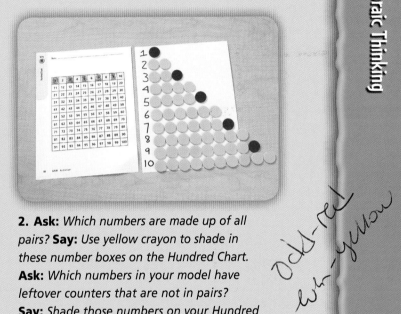

2. Ask: *Which numbers are made up of all pairs?* **Say:** *Use yellow crayon to shade in these number boxes on the Hundred Chart.* **Ask:** *Which numbers in your model have leftover counters that are not in pairs?* **Say:** *Shade those numbers on your Hundred Chart with red crayon.*

⚠ Look Out!

Watch for children who think numbers ending in zero are neither even nor odd. Have them skip-count by 2s from 2 to 30 and note the numbers that end in zero.

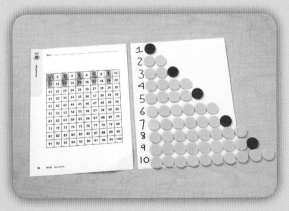

3. Ask: *What pattern do you see on the Hundred Chart?* **Say:** *Use the pattern to complete the chart.*

Use Two-Color Counters. Build each number in the rows. Write the number. Circle all odd numbers. (Check students' work.)

1.

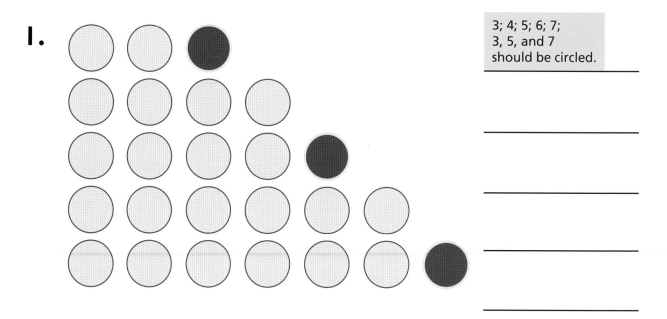

3; 4; 5; 6; 7;
3, 5, and 7
should be circled.

Use Two-Color Counters. Build each number. Circle the number if it is odd.

2. 11

Check students' models; number should be circled.

3. 14

Check students' models; number should not be circled

For each number, write odd or even.

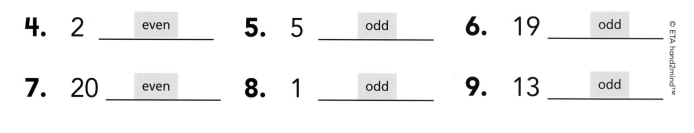

4. 2 _____ even

5. 5 _____ odd

6. 19 _____ odd

7. 20 _____ even

8. 1 _____ odd

9. 13 _____ odd

Download student pages at hand2mind.com/hosstudent.

Challenge! What digits can be in the ones place for a number to be even?

Challenge: 0, 2, 4, 6, and 8

_____

_____

_____

_____

_____

_____

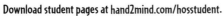

© ETA hand2mind™

Repeated Addition

LESSON

4

Objective

Relate multiplication to repeated addition.

Common Core State Standards

■ **2.OA.4** Use addition to find the total number of objects arranged in rectangular arrays with up to 5 rows and up to 5 columns; write an equation to express the total as a sum of equal addends.

When multiplication is introduced to children as repeated addition, it is not a "new" process, but an expansion of a familiar one. Repeated addition combines identical number groups, for example, 3 + 3 + 3. Multiplication also combines identical number groups, but is more efficient. Children should learn the differences between these two operations while appreciating the equality of the answers.

Try It! *Perform the Try It! activity on the next page.*

Talk About It

Discuss the Try It! activity.

■ Have children look at their completed Color Tile Arrays 1 and 2 worksheets (BLM 4, BLM 5). Direct them to Exercise 1. **Ask:** *How many rows are there? How many tiles are in each row? Does each row have exactly the same number of tiles?*

■ **Ask:** *How did you use addition to find the number in all?* Invite children to explain how to use repeated addition to find the total number of tiles in the array. Repeat the questions for other exercises on the worksheets.

Solve It

With children, reread the problem. Play an array game like the one described in the problem. For example, **say:** *3 rows with 6 tiles in each row.* Have children build the array and find the number in all. Then invite volunteers to tell how they used repeated addition to find the answer.

More Ideas

For other ways to teach relating multiplication to repeated addition—

■ Have pairs of children use Two-Color Counters to model and solve repeated addition problems. For example, **say:** *Tara saw 2 birds on a tree, 2 birds in a birdbath, and 2 birds on a bird feeder.* **Ask:** *How many birds did Tara see in all?* Have children write an addition sentence (2 + 2 + 2 = 6), and complete this sentence: [3] groups of [2] is [6].

■ Have children set out 5 trapezoid Pattern Blocks, cover them with triangle blocks, and find the total number of triangles. Then have them write the addition sentence (3 + 3 + 3 + 3 + 3 = 15) and complete this sentence: [5] groups of [3] triangle blocks is [15].

Formative Assessment

Have children try the following problem.

Circle the number sentence that matches the tiles.

A. 4 + 4 + 4 = 12   **B.** 2 + 2 = 4   **C.** 3 + 3 + 3 = 9

Try It! 30 minutes | Pairs

Here is a problem about relating multiplication to repeated addition.

José is playing a game during math club. José's teacher describes a Color Tile array by calling out the number of rows and the number of tiles in each row. Then one child finds the total number of tiles in the array. How can José use the number of rows and the number of tiles in each row to find the number of tiles in all when it's his turn?

Introduce the problem. Then have children do the activity to solve the problem.

Distribute tiles and copies of the Color Tile Arrays 1 and 2 (BLM 4, BLM 5) to children.

Materials
- Color Tiles (50 assorted tiles per pair)
- Color Tile Arrays 1 (BLM 4; 1 per child)
- Color Tile Arrays 2 (BLM 5; 1 per child)

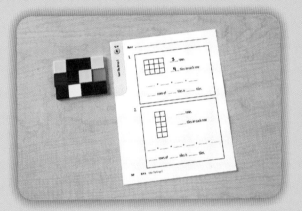

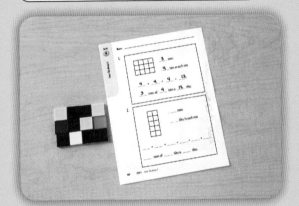

1. Ask: *What do we do when we see the words "in all"? How can we find the number of tiles in all?* Guide children to conclude that they should add. Then instruct children to look at the first array on the worksheet. Have children use their tiles to model the same array. **Ask:** *How many rows are in this array? How many tiles are in each row?* Have children write the correct numbers next to the first array.

2. Explain to children that to find the answer (the number of tiles in all), they need to add the number of tiles in each row (4) 3 times. Have children complete the addition sentence on their Color Tile Arrays 1 worksheet. Then have them complete the final sentence for the exercise by filling in the number of rows and tiles and the number in all.

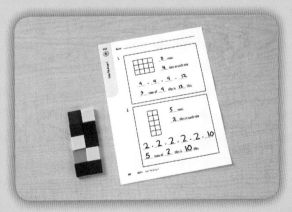

3. Have children repeat steps 1 and 2 to complete Exercises 2 through 4 on the Color Tile Arrays 1 and 2 worksheets.

⚠ Look Out!

Watch out for children who try to add the number of rows instead of adding the number of tiles in each row. Encourage these children to count the number of tiles in row 1 and write that number in the addition sentence, then the number of tiles in row 2, and so on until they have filled in the addition sentence. It might also help these children to build their arrays with a different color for each row. That way, they will more easily see the arrangement of a group of tiles in one row.

Use Color Tiles. Make each model.
Fill in the blanks.

1.

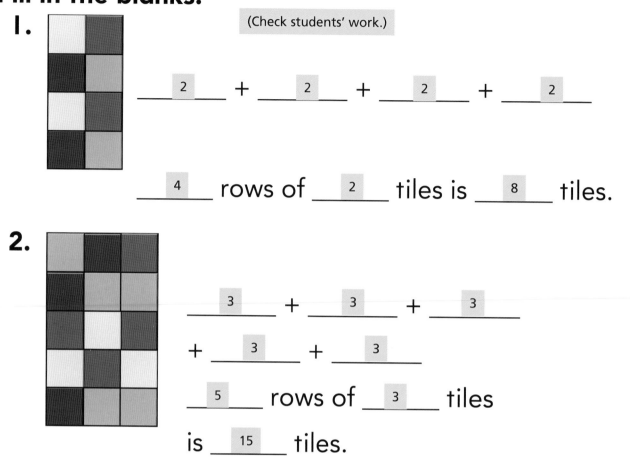

(Check students' work.)

_____2_____ + _____2_____ + _____2_____ + _____2_____

_____4_____ rows of _____2_____ tiles is _____8_____ tiles.

2.

_____3_____ + _____3_____ + _____3_____

+ _____3_____ + _____3_____

_____5_____ rows of _____3_____ tiles

is _____15_____ tiles.

Use Color Tiles. Make a 4 × 5 array.
Draw the model. Fill in the blanks.

3.

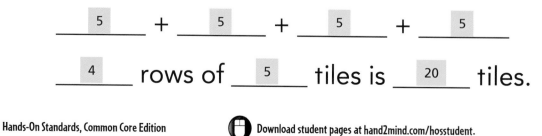

_____5_____ + _____5_____ + _____5_____ + _____5_____

_____4_____ rows of _____5_____ tiles is _____20_____ tiles.

Download student pages at hand2mind.com/hosstudent.

© ETA hand2mind™

Challenge! What repeated addition does

6×2 represent?

Challenge: $2 + 2 + 2 + 2 + 2 + 2 = 12$

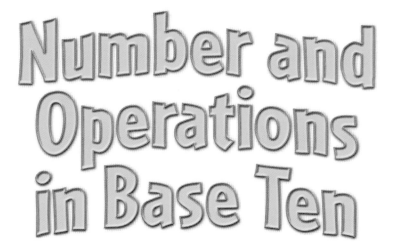

Number and Operations in Base Ten

In second grade, children extend their base ten learning to hundreds. They understand that the three digits of a three-digit number represent amounts of hundreds, tens, and ones and that 100 is the same amount as 10 groups of ten as well as 100 ones.

Children explore and discuss number patterns as they count within 1,000 by "counting on" from any number and skip-counting by 5s, 10s, and 100s. They read and write numbers to 1,000 using base ten numerals, number names, and expanded form. They compare two three-digit numbers based on the meanings of the hundreds, tens, and ones digits and use >, <, and = symbols to record the results of comparisons after having sufficient experience communicating about the comparisons with words.

In second grade, children fluently add and subtract within 100 by using strategies that make sense to them involving place value, properties of operations, and/or the relationship between addition and subtraction. They begin working with concrete models, drawings, and additional strategies to add and subtract within 1,000. Children understand that when adding or subtracting three-digit numbers it is sometimes necessary to compose or decompose tens and/or hundreds, but the standard algorithm of carrying or borrowing is not an expectation in second grade.

The Grade 2 Common Core State Standards for Number and Operations in Base Ten specify that children should–

- Understand place value.
- Use place value understanding and properties of operations to add and subtract.

The following hands-on activities provide opportunities for children to use manipulatives and picture representations to make connections in the base ten number system. Children are called to explain why addition and subtraction strategies work, and use place value and the properties of operations. Children may use drawings or objects to support their explanations. The experiences with manipulatives will lead toward proficiency applying strategies to solve addition and subtraction problems.

Number and Operations in Base Ten
Contents

Objective

Understand a 3-digit number in terms of hundreds, tens, and ones.

Common Core State Standards

- **2.NBT.1a** Understand that 100 can be thought of as a bundle of ten tens — called a "hundred."

- **2.NBT.1b** Understand that the numbers 100, 200, 300, 400, 500, 600, 700, 800, 900 refer to one, two, three, four, five, six, seven, eight, or nine hundreds (and 0 tens and 0 ones).

Number and Operations in Base Ten

Three-Digit Numbers

To work with three-digit numbers and to find three-digit sums, children need to extend their understanding of place value to the hundreds place. They must understand the idea that 10 tens make one hundred, and they should learn to think flexibly about a hundred as either a single entity or ten separate tens, depending on the situation. With this understanding, children are prepared to learn further that a three-digit number can have one, two, three, four, five, six, seven, eight, or nine hundreds.

Try It! Perform the Try It! activity on the next page.

Talk About It

Discuss the Try It! activity.

- **Ask:** *How many rods are equal to one flat? How many tens are equal to one hundred?* **Say:** *100 can be thought of as a bundle of 10 tens.* Write the number *106* and point to the three digits. Discuss how the digits represent the place values on the place-value chart and how the zero in 106 shows that there are no tens.

- **Ask:** *If Nate bought a second pack of 10 cards, how many cards would he have? Discuss how another 10 cards would make a total of 116 cards.*

- **Ask:** *If Nate bought 10 more packs of cards, how many cards would he have?* Discuss how another 10 tens would make another hundred, for a total of 216 cards.

Solve It

With children, reread the problem. Have children draw the Base Ten Blocks for 96, for another 10, and for the total, exchanging 10 rods for a flat. Have children write the number sentence for the problem, 96 + 10 = 106.

More Ideas

For other ways to teach place value in three-digit numbers—

- Have pairs use a spinner to spin 3 numerals. Have them write the three numerals as a three-digit number and build the number using Base Ten Blocks. Have them identify the value of each digit.

- Have children use Base Ten Blocks to build the numbers 100, 200, 300, 400, 500, 600, 700, 800, and 900. Have them explain these numbers as different amounts of hundreds.

Formative Assessment

Have children try the following problem.

Which number is shown with the blocks?

A. 710   **B.** 701   **C.** 170

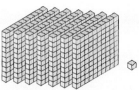

Try It! 20 minutes | Pairs

Here is a problem about place value in three-digit numbers.

Nate collects trading cards. He had 96 trading cards. Then he bought another pack of 10 cards. How many trading cards does Nate have now?

Introduce the problem. Then have children do the activity to solve the problem. Distribute Base Ten Blocks and a Place-Value Chart (BLM 6) to children.

Materials
- Base Ten Blocks (5 flats, 20 rods, and 10 units per pair)
- Place-Value Chart (BLM 6; 1 per pair)
- pencils (1 per pair)

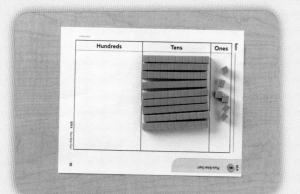

1. Say: *Nate had 96 trading cards.* **Ask:** *How can you show 96 using Base Ten Blocks? How many tens are in 96? How many ones are in 96?* Have children count out 9 rods and 6 units and place them in the Tens and Ones columns on their charts.

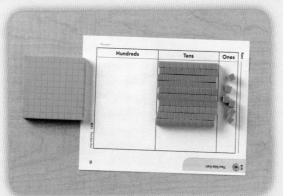

2. Say: *Nate bought another pack of 10 cards.* **Ask:** *What should you add to your blocks to show the new pack of 10? How many rods do you have now?* **Say:** *Push your 10 rods together and compare them to a hundred flat.* Elicit that the 10 rods are the same as a flat.

⚠ Look Out!

Watch for children who aren't making the connection between the sizes of the Base Ten Blocks and the place-value positions in the numbers. Remind them that the bigger blocks go on the left and that the blocks get smaller going to the right, just like the numbers when we read them.

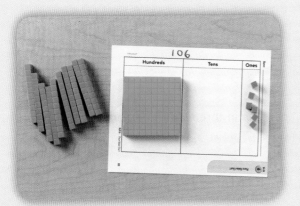

3. Have children exchange 10 rods for one flat and place the flat in the Hundreds column of their chart. **Ask:** *How many flats do you have? How many rods do you have? How many units do you have?* **Say:** *We can write this number as 1 hundred, 0 tens, 6 ones.*

Use Base Ten Blocks. Build each number. Write the number. (Check students' work.)

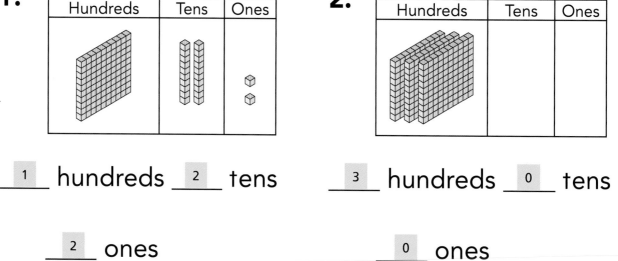

1.

Hundreds	Tens	Ones

___1___ hundreds ___2___ tens

___2___ ones

2.

Hundreds	Tens	Ones

___3___ hundreds ___0___ tens

___0___ ones

Use Base Ten Blocks. Build each number. Draw the model. Write the number.

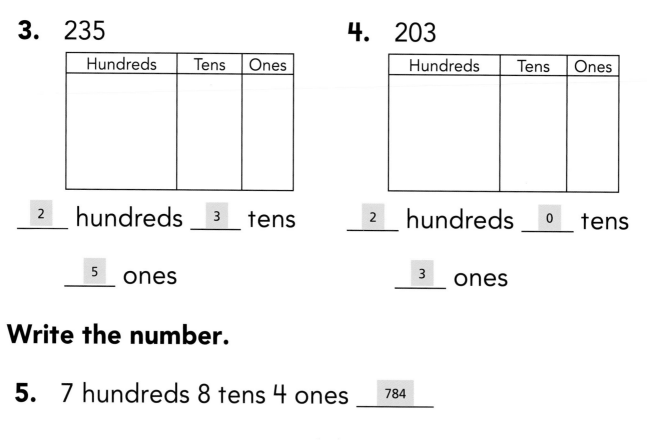

3. 235

Hundreds	Tens	Ones

___2___ hundreds ___3___ tens

___5___ ones

4. 203

Hundreds	Tens	Ones

___2___ hundreds ___0___ tens

___3___ ones

Write the number.

5. 7 hundreds 8 tens 4 ones ___784___

Challenge!   The library had 850 books. They bought 100 more books. How many books does the library have now? Use Base Ten Blocks. Build the numbers. Draw the blocks. Write how many in all.

Challenge: Drawing should show 8 flats and 5 rods for 850 and 1 flat for 100; 950 books.

_____

_____

_____

_____

_____

_____

Number and Operations in Base Ten

Skip-Counting by 5s

It is important for teachers to offer children opportunities to make generalizations about observations they make while exploring mathematical situations. Using a hundred chart allows children to organize information in an easy-to-follow visual model. As children explore skip-counting, they begin to see a relationship between number patterns and operations. As they begin connecting the two, they form the basis of algebraic thinking.

Try It! Perform the Try It! activity on the next page.

Talk About It

Discuss the Try It! activity.

■ **Ask:** *What do you notice about the numbers in each column you marked with a 2-cm Color Cube?* Guide children to conclude that they all end in 0 or 5.

■ **Ask:** *When might we use skip-counting by 5s?*

■ **Ask:** *How is skip-counting by 5s the same as skip-counting by 2s? How is it different? How is skip-counting by 10 different from skip-counting by 5? How is it the same? Can you rewrite the problem so that it uses skip-counting by 10? by 2?*

Solve It

With children, reread the problem. Have them explain in writing how Terra can use skip-counting by 5s on a Hundred Chart to find the total number of chairs.

More Ideas

For other ways to teach about skip-counting by 5s—

■ Have children use Snap Cubes® to make 10 trains of 5 cubes each. Have them touch each train as they skip-count by 5s and say the numbers aloud.

■ Have children use 2-cm Color Cubes and a Hundred Chart (BLM 2) to skip-count by 10s and mark those with a green cube. Then skip-count by 5s and mark those with a yellow cube. Have children put a yellow cube on top of a green cube where both numbers occur together. Have children compare the two patterns.

■ Have children use Two-Color Counters and a Hundred Chart to count by 5s, but start on 12. **Ask:** *What happened to the number pattern we saw when we started at 1?*

Formative Assessment

Have children try the following problem.

Complete the pattern.

0, 5, 10, 15, _____, _____, _____.

Try It! 20 minutes | Groups of 3

Here is a problem about skip-counting by 5s.

In Terra's classroom, there are 4 tables. Each table has 5 chairs. How could Terra find the total number of chairs without counting each chair one by one?

Introduce the problem. Then have the children do the activity to solve the problem.

Give 2-cm Color Cubes, a Hundred Chart (BLM 2), and a crayon to each group.

1. Have children count by 1s to 5, then place a color cube on the number 5 on the Hundred Chart. **Ask:** *If we count 5 more, what number would we land on?* Children should count 5 more on the Hundred Chart and then place a cube on the 10. Have children continue to count 5 more and place a cube on every fifth number until they reach 20.

2. Have one group member recount by touching the marked numbers and saying just the fifth numbers aloud. Have another group member remove the cubes one at a time and use the crayon to circle those numbers on the Hundred Chart.

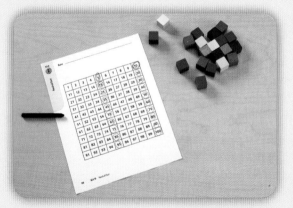

3. Ask children to describe the pattern they see in the numbers. Have children work in groups to place the rest of the cubes on the chart, completing the number pattern to skip-count by 5s to 100. Then have two groups race. One group counts to 20 by 1s, and the other group counts by 5s. **Ask:** *Which group reached 20 first?*

⚠ Look Out!

For children who need more help understanding skip-counting, draw a number line with 20 numbers. Circle the 5s and mark Xs through the other numbers. Explain that when you skip-count, you "skip" over certain numbers.

Use 2-cm Color Cubes and a Hundred Chart. Make the chart shown. Write the numbers of the skip-counting.

(Check students' work.)

1.

1	2	3	4		6	7	8	9	
11	12	13	14		16	17	18	19	
21	22	23	24		26	27	28	29	
31	32	33	34		36	37	38	39	

_5_, _10_, _15_, _20_, _25_, _30_, _35_, _40_

Model skip-counting by 5. The starting number is given. Write numbers in the blanks.

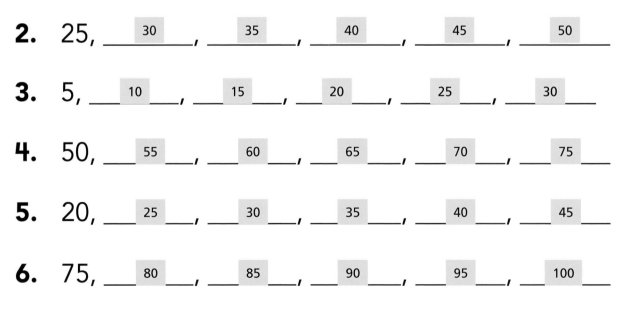

2. 25, _30_, _35_, _40_, _45_, _50_

3. 5, _10_, _15_, _20_, _25_, _30_

4. 50, _55_, _60_, _65_, _70_, _75_

5. 20, _25_, _30_, _35_, _40_, _45_

6. 75, _80_, _85_, _90_, _95_, _100_

© ETA hand2mind™

Challenge! When you skip-count by 5, what digits are in the ones place of the numbers you say? Draw a picture to help.

Challenge: (Sample) 0 and 5

_____

_____

_____

_____

_____

© ETA hand2mind™

Represent Numbers

Representing numbers in multiple and flexible ways helps children gain number sense. Often children will understand one representation of a number, such as a numeral, but not a physical representation, such as with Base Ten Blocks. Using multiple representations of a number in the classroom reinforces the concept of a number. Understanding multiple representations sets the stage for algebraic thinking in which children will be able to identify a variable as a representation of a number.

Try It! *Perform the Try It! activity on the next page.*

Talk About It

Discuss the Try It! activity.

- Have children discuss how they know that different representations of the same number are equal.

- **Ask:** *How could you show the number 11? What are two ways to show this number? What if we changed to the number 9? What are two ways you could show that number?*

Solve It

With children, reread the problem. Invite them to use crayons and paper to make a poster that shows Steven's age four different ways. Tell children that they can draw a picture of a model for one of the ways.

More Ideas

For other ways to teach about representing the numbers 1 to 12 in different forms—

- Have children grab handfuls of Color Tiles. Then have children count the tiles, write the number, and show the number in two other ways.

- Have children write a number and word name and represent the number using Snap Cubes®.

Formative Assessment

Have children try the following problem.

Which picture shows 12? Draw a circle around the picture.

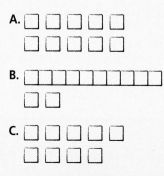

Objective

Represent numbers 1 to 12 in different forms.

Common Core State Standards

- **2.NBT.3** Read and write numbers to 1000 using base-ten numerals, number names, and expanded form.

Try It!   15 minutes | Groups of 4

Here is a problem about representing the numbers 1 to 12 in different forms.

Steven is Jim's older brother. He just turned 11 years old. Mr. Anton, Jim's teacher, asked the class to make a birthday poster for Steven to show his age in four different ways. How can the class show Steven's age in four different ways?

Introduce the problem. Then have children do the activity to solve the problem.

Before children do the activity, ask them to give examples of ways in which they might want to show an amount by using a word, a number, a tally mark, or a model (such as Base Ten Blocks). Give out blocks, counters, index cards, and crayons. **Say:** *Let's show the same number in different ways.*

Materials
- Base Ten Blocks (1 rod and 12 units per group)
- Two-Color Counters (11 per group)
- index cards (3 per group)
- crayons (3 per group)

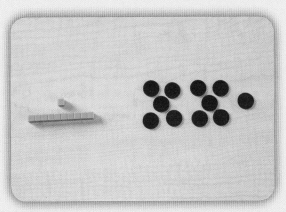

1. To begin, say the number 11 out loud. Give the blocks to one child in each group and the counters to another. Give index cards and crayons to the other children. Ask the two children to use the blocks and counters to model two ways to show 11.

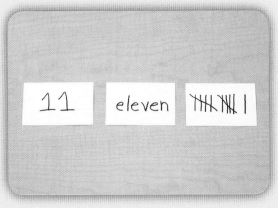

2. Ask the children with the index cards to work together to show 11 in three other ways. For example, children can make 11 tally marks, write the number 11, and write the word *eleven*.

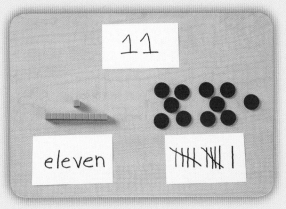

3. Ask groups to check that all representations show the same number.

⚠ Look Out!

Check that children have created multiple representations of the same number. Children need to realize that the Base Ten rod equals and can be exchanged for 10 units.

Use Two-Color Counters and Base Ten Blocks. Build the sets shown. Complete each sentence.

(Check students' work.)

1.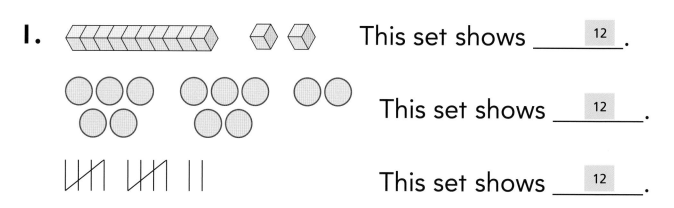

This set shows ____12____.

This set shows ____12____.

This set shows ____12____.

Use Two-Color Counters and Base Ten Blocks. Draw a picture for each number.

Check students' drawings.

2. 9

Two-Color Counters:

Base Ten Blocks:

Tally Marks:

3. 10

Two-Color Counters:

Base Ten Blocks:

Tally Marks:

Challenge! Besides using Two-Color Counters, Base Ten Blocks, and Tally Marks, what are other ways to show a number?

Challenge: (Sample) Digits, words, sets of other objects

_____

_____

_____

_____

_____

_____

© ETA hand2mind™

Objective

Write numbers in different forms.

Common Core State Standards

■ **2.NBT.3** Read and write numbers to 1000 using base-ten numerals, number names, and expanded form.

Number and Operations in Base Ten

Numbers in Different Forms

For children to have confidence about numbers and their meanings, it is important that they understand different representations of numbers, including base ten numerals, number names, and expanded forms. The ability to represent and recognize numbers in different forms enables children to exercise a deeper understanding of number, and this serves as a strong foundation for children when they add and subtract two- and three-digit numbers.

Try It! *Perform the Try It! activity on the next page.*

Talk About It

Discuss the Try It! activity.

■ **Ask:** *How does understanding place value help you show numbers in different ways?* Discuss how knowing place value makes building numbers with Base Ten Blocks easier, how it makes breaking numbers apart for expanded form easier, and how it makes writing numbers in word form easier.

■ **Ask:** *How did you write 642 in expanded form? How did you know how to separate the different parts of 642 when you wrote it in expanded form and in word form?*

■ **Say:** *There are many ways to represent numbers. Each way is useful in certain situations.*

Solve It

With children, reread the problem. Have children review their recording sheet for 642. **Say:** *Let's say Amy's brother wanted to show the number 769 in four ways.* Have children complete a new copy of the Number Forms Recording Sheet (BLM 7) for 769.

More Ideas

For other ways to teach writing numbers in different forms—

■ Have pairs of children play a number game. One child says a number and the other child shows that number using Base Ten Blocks, expanded form, or word form. Have children check each other's work, and then switch roles.

■ Have children spin a 0–9 spinner three times and write the digits on their paper in any order. Have them write the expanded form and word form of the number.

Formative Assessment

Have children try the following problem.

Which shows the expanded form of 769?

A. 70 + 60 + 9   **B.** 700 + 60 + 90   **C.** 700 + 60 + 9

Try It! 30 minutes | Groups of 4

Here is a problem about writing numbers in different forms.

Amy and her younger brother were talking about numbers. Her brother thought the only way to show 642 was to write it as a numeral. Amy told her brother there are other ways to show the number. What are 3 other ways to show 642?

Introduce the problem. Then have children do the activity to solve the problem. Distribute Base Ten Blocks, recording sheets, and pencils to children.

Materials

- Base Ten Blocks (10 flats, 10 rods, and 10 units per group)
- Number Forms Recording Sheet (BLM 7; 1 per child)
- pencils (1 per child)

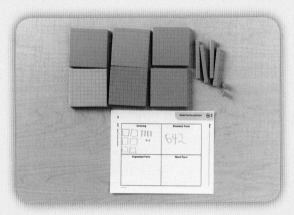

1. Say: *You can use the blocks to build a model of the number.* **Ask:** *Which blocks would you use?* Discuss how to show the number using Base Ten Blocks. Have children draw the blocks they used to model the number and write the number in standard form on their recording sheets.

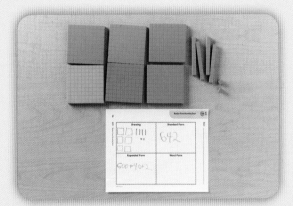

2. Say: *The blocks help us show 642 another way. Think about what each digit means.* Elicit that the 6 flats represent 600, the 4 rods represent 40, and the 2 units represent 2. Write *600 + 40 + 2* on the board, have children write it on their recording sheets, and tell children that it is the expanded form of 642.

⚠ Look Out!

Watch for children who aren't going from blocks to expanded form easily. Have them look at each type of block separately and write what those blocks total. Remind them to use plus signs between the numbers to indicate that the parts are put together.

3. Ask: *How would we write 642 using words?* Discuss the place values of the digits and write *six hundred forty-two* on the board. **Say:** *This is the word form of the number. Write it on your sheet.*

Use Base Ten Blocks. Build each number. Write the number in expanded form and standard form.

(Check students' work.)

1.

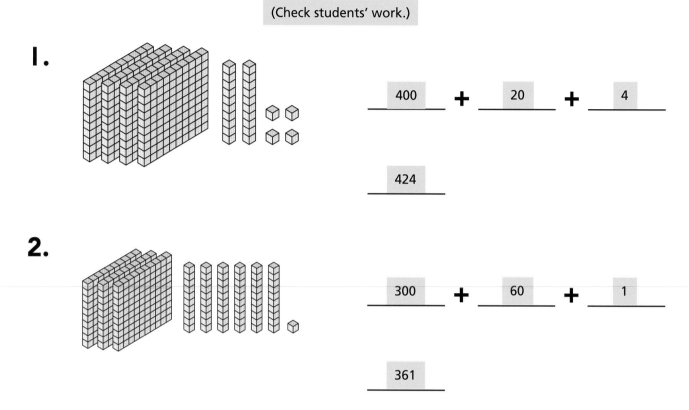

_____400_____ **+** _____20_____ **+** _____4_____

_____424_____

2.

_____300_____ **+** _____60_____ **+** _____1_____

_____361_____

Use Base Ten Blocks. Build the number. Draw the model. Write the number in standard form.

3. two hundred fifty-seven

_____2 flats, 5 rods, 7 units; 257_____

Write each number.

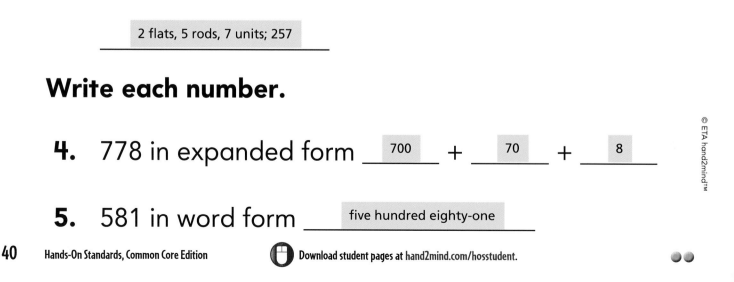

4. 778 in expanded form _____700_____ **+** _____70_____ **+** _____8_____

5. 581 in word form _____five hundred eighty-one_____

Challenge! Sarah saw *three hundred five* written on a paper. She wrote the number as 305. Her brother George said that since there is no zero in the number name, there should not be one in the number. Who is right, Sarah or George? Use words and drawings to explain.

Challenge: (Sample) Sarah is correct because the zero is needed to hold the tens place, even though there are no tens.

© ETA hand2mind™

Objective

Compare 3-digit numbers.

Common Core State Standards

■ **2.NBT.4** Compare two three-digit numbers based on meanings of the hundreds, tens, and ones digits, using >, =, and < symbols to record the results of comparisons.

Number and Operations in Base Ten

Comparing Three-Digit Numbers

Comparing quantities helps children develop number sense, and the ability to compare is essential in problem solving. Children need opportunities to connect quantities with the numerals that represent them. Hands-on learning experiences, such as using Base Ten Blocks, provide these opportunities and help children gain proficiency in comparing, both visually and mentally. Applying the symbols >, <, and = allows children to practice using symbols to represent mathematical ideas.

Try It! *Perform the Try It! activity on the next page.*

Talk About It

Discuss the Try It! activity.

■ Write the numbers *748* and *673* on the board. **Ask:** *Where do I look first to find out which number is greater? Which number is greater? How can you tell?*

■ Write the numbers *561* and *556* on the board. **Say:** *These numbers have the same number in the hundreds place.* **Ask:** *Where should I look to find out which number is greater?*

■ Write *561 > 556*. **Ask:** *Can you write another statement about these numbers using the < sign?*

Solve It

With children, reread the problem. Have children write the numbers for each boy's pile of blocks and complete the number sentence. Then have children write a sentence comparing the two numbers.

More Ideas

For other ways to teach comparing three-digit numbers—

■ Have pairs use a spinner to spin 3 numbers, and have each child create a three-digit number using the 3 numbers spun. Have children use the numbers they created and write two number sentences using < or >. Children can use Base Ten Blocks to model and check the answers to their sentences.

■ Have children pick 3 digits out of a bag. Have one child make the greatest number and the other child make the least number that can be made from the three digits. Then have pairs use > or < to write two sentences comparing the numbers. Children can use Base Ten Blocks to model and check the answers to their sentences.

Formative Assessment

Have children try the following problem.

Which number makes this true?

_____ *< 407*

A. 704 **B.** 470 **C.** 401

Try It! 20 minutes | Pairs

Here is a problem about comparing three-digit numbers.

Ali and Jafar each have a pile of Base Ten Blocks. Ali says his blocks make a greater number than Jafar's blocks. Jafar says his blocks make a greater number. Ali has 8 units, 2 flats, and 2 rods. Jafar has 4 units, 2 flats, and 3 rods. Use Ali's and Jafar's numbers to make this number sentence true: _____ > _____.

Introduce the problem. Then have children do the activity to solve the problem. Distribute Base Ten Blocks, charts, index cards, and pencils to children.

Materials
- Base Ten Blocks (10 flats, 10 rods, and 20 units per pair)
- Place-Value Chart (BLM 6; 2 per pair)
- index cards (2 per pair)
- pencils (2 per pair)

1. Say: *Let's make the two piles of blocks first.*
Ask: *How many flats does each boy have? How many rods? How many units?* Have one child be Jafar and the other be Ali. Have each child build his or her pile of blocks.

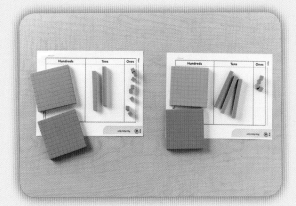

2. Have each child place his or her blocks on a chart to model the number the blocks represent. **Say:** *Let's compare the numbers.* Elicit that the hundreds place is compared first because it is the greatest. Explain that since the models have the same number of hundreds, the comparison has to move to the tens.

⚠ Look Out!

Watch for children who aren't comparing each place value correctly. Make sure they are looking at each value position separately to make a valid comparison. Some pairs might benefit from putting the place-value charts one under the other and lining up the columns to make a better comparison.

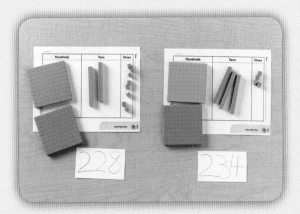

3. Ask: *Which number has more tens? Which number is greater?* Write _____ > _____ on the board. **Say:** *Use the numbers to make this number sentence true.* Discuss the meanings of > and <, have each child write his or her number on an index card, and have pairs complete the number sentence.

Use Base Ten Blocks. Build each number. Compare the numbers. Write the numbers with < or > between them. (Check students' work.)

I.

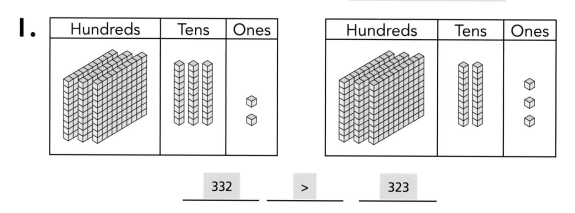

Hundreds	Tens	Ones

___332___ ___>___ ___323___

Build each number. Draw the models. Write the numbers with < or > between them.

2. 235   330

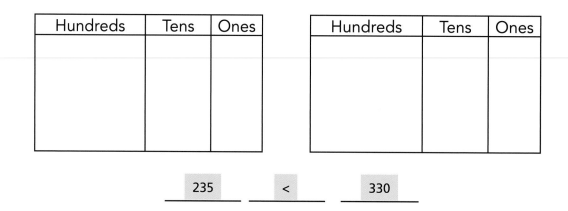

Hundreds	Tens	Ones

___235___ ___<___ ___330___

Write < or > between the numbers.

3. 636 ___<___ 663   **4.** 178 ___>___ 175

Challenge! Rosa has 5 flats, 7 rods, and 4 units on her desk. Irene says her blocks show the same number, but Irene has 5 flats and 6 rods. How many units would Irene have to have to equal Rosa's blocks? Draw the models of Rosa's and Irene's blocks. Write a sentence to explain.

Challenge: Irene would have to have 14 units.

_____

_____

_____

_____

_____

_____

Objective

Add 2-digit numbers.

Common Core State Standards

- **2.NBT.6** Add up to four two-digit numbers using strategies based on place value and properties of operations.

Number and Operations in Base Ten

Adding Two-Digit Numbers

To facilitate adding more than 2 two-digit numbers, children need to use the various properties of addition. For example, understanding that changing the order of the numbers added does not change the sum will help children regroup the numbers to find easy sums. Using concrete objects to add helps children internalize the necessary concepts.

Try It! *Perform the Try It! activity on the next page.*

Talk About It

Discuss the Try It! activity.

- **Say:** *You also can begin by adding 70 + 72. You can add the ones: 2 + 0, and then the tens: 7 + 7.* **Ask:** *How many ones do you have? (2) What is the total of your tens? (140)* **Say:** *Now you can add 140 + 2 to get 142.*

- **Say:** *Now you add 142 + 68. This also has easy numbers to group together. You can add the ones: 2 + 8, and then the tens: 140 + 60.* **Ask:** *What is 2 + 8? (10) What is 140 + 60? (200)* **Say:** *You can now add 200 + 10 to get 210 people.*

Solve It

With children, reread the problem. Have children write the number of people from each night as an addition problem: 68 + 70 + 72 = ___. Have children circle the numbers they grouped together, connect with a line, and write the total underneath the line. Then have them add the remaining number and write the total number of people at the soccer games.

More Ideas

For other ways to teach adding 3 or 4 two-digit numbers—

- Write several addition problems with 3 or 4 two-digit numbers on note cards and allow children to select cards at random. Have children rewrite the addition problems vertically on paper, grouping the numbers that are easily added, and model them with Base Ten Blocks. Remind children to look for easy numbers to add—those that equal ten or involve adding zero. Have them write the total.

- Have children pick 3 or 4 two-digit numbers from a bag. Ask them to group the numbers into easy ways to add. Have children use Base Ten Blocks to help them visualize how the groupings can help them solve the problems.

Formative Assessment

Have children try the following problem.

Which numbers can be grouped to add more easily?

82 + 19 + 31 + 47

A. 82 + 47   **B.** 82 + 19   **C.** 19 + 31

Try It! 25 minutes | Groups of 3

Here is a problem about adding more than 2 two-digit numbers.

Marisol wanted to know how many people came to the soccer games over three nights. On Monday night, there were 68 people. On Tuesday night, there were 70 people. On Thursday night, there were 72 people. How can Marisol easily add these three numbers to find the total number of people?

Introduce the problem. Then have children do the activity to solve the problem. Distribute Base Ten Blocks, paper, and pencils to children.

Materials

- Base Ten Blocks (5 flats, 25 rods, and 20 units per group)
- paper (1 sheet per group)
- pencils (1 per group)

1. Say: *Let's write the numbers we need to add.* Write 68 + 70 + 72. Have children build each number using Base Ten Blocks. **Ask:** *Do you notice any numbers that might be easier to add?* Generate a discussion about adding 68 + 72 (since 8 + 2 = 10) or 70 + 72 (since 7 + 7 = 14).

2. Say: *We can group 68 and 72 to add the ones easily. Use your blocks to add the ones.* **Ask:** *How many ones do you have? How can you regroup those ones into tens?* **Say:** *Place all the tens together.*

⚠ Look Out!

Watch for children who aren't grouping numbers for easier addition. Help them focus just on the ones or the tens to find numbers that are easiest to add. Adding any number to zero is always easy, and finding numbers that will have a sum of 10 also makes adding easier.

3. Say: *Now let's add these tens to the remaining number of people.* **Ask:** *How many tens do you have? How many hundred flats can you trade for? How many people came to the soccer games?*

Use Base Ten Blocks. Build the numbers.
Group the numbers. Add. (Check students' work.)

I. 27 + 30 + 43 = _27 + 43 = 70, 70 + 30 = 100_

Use Base Ten Blocks. Build the numbers.
Group the numbers. Draw the groups. Add.

2. 17 + 49 + 23 + 11 = 17 + 23 = 40, 49 + 11 = 60, 40 + 60 = 100

Add.

3. 55 + 60 + 15 + 20 = 55 + 15 = 70, 60 + 20 = 80, 80 + 70 = 150

4. 54 + 76 + 40 = _54 + 76 = 130, 130 + 40 = 170_

5. 16 + 22 + 80 + 52 = 16 + 22 = 38, 38 + 52 = 90, 90 + 80 = 170

 Download student pages at hand2mind.com/hosstudent.

Challenge!   Alex and Anthony added the points the basketball team scored in four games. The team scored 48 points, 43 points, 52 points, and 37 points. Alex wants to add 43 + 37 and then 48 + 52. Anthony wants to add 48 + 43 and then 52 + 37. Which boy is adding the points in the easier way? Explain why, and then show the sum.

Challenge: (Sample) Answers will vary, but most children will say Alex is grouping the numbers to make easier addends: 3 + 7 = 10 and 8 + 2 = 10. Then all he has to do is add the tens. The sum is 180.

_____

_____

_____

_____

_____

_____

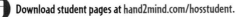

© ETA hand2mind™

Objective

Add and subtract within 1,000.

Common Core State Standards

■ **2.NBT.7** Add and subtract within 1000, using concrete models or drawings and strategies based on place value, properties of operations, and/ or the relationship between addition and subtraction; relate the strategy to a written method. Understand that in adding or subtracting three-digit numbers, one adds or subtracts hundreds and hundreds, tens and tens, ones and ones; and sometimes it is necessary to compose or decompose tens or hundreds.

Number and Operations in Base Ten

Adding and Subtracting Within 1,000

Adding and subtracting multi-digit numbers is an important skill in everyday life. Addition and subtraction require children to represent numbers and understand their values. Children will use their prior knowledge in place value, comparing three-digit numbers, and properties of operations to add and subtract numbers within 1,000, with and without regrouping.

Try It! Perform the Try It! activity on the next page.

Talk About It

Discuss the Try It! activity.

■ Write *253* and *324* on the board. **Ask:** *What is the best way to write these numbers as an addition problem?* Help children set up the addition vertically and realize they must align the place-value columns.

■ **Say:** *Remember that when you add, you sometimes need to regroup.* **Ask:** *How do you know when you need to regroup? Are there any numbers you need to regroup in this problem? How do you show regrouping using your blocks?* Add the numbers together as a class.

■ **Say:** *You may need to regroup when you are subtracting, too.* **Ask:** *Do you need to regroup any numbers when you are subtracting in this problem? What do you need to do with your blocks when you regroup to subtract? How is regrouping different for adding than it is for subtracting?*

Solve It

With children, reread the problem. Have children draw blocks and write two number sentences to find the total number of problems that Dawn and Lina solved and how many problems David and Zac solved.

More Ideas

For another way to teach adding and subtracting within 1,000—

■ Have pairs pick 6 numbers out of a bag to make 2 three-digit numbers. Have one child add them and the other child subtract the smaller number from the larger number.

Formative Assessment

Have children try the following problem.

$$\begin{array}{r} 245 \\ + 127 \\ \hline \end{array}$$

A. 122   **B.** 362   **C.** 372

Try It! 30 minutes | Groups of 3

Here is a problem about adding and subtracting within 1,000.

Dawn, Lina, David, and Zac are keeping track of the number of math problems they solve. So far, Dawn has solved 253 problems and Lina has solved 354 problems. David and Zac have solved 89 fewer problems than Dawn and Lina. How many problems have David and Zac solved?

Introduce the problem. Then have children do the activity to solve the problem. Distribute Base Ten Blocks, charts, and pencils to children.

Materials
- Base Ten Blocks (10 flats, 20 rods, and 20 units per group)
- Triple Place-Value Chart (BLM 8; 2 per child)
- pencils (1 per child)

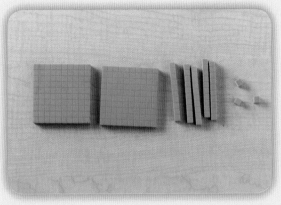

1. Say: *First we will add together 253 and 354. Show 253 with blocks. Draw the blocks you used on the chart and draw a plus sign below them.* Have children set the blocks they used to the side.

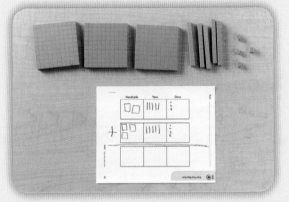

2. Say: *Now we will use new blocks to show 354.* Have children build the number and then draw the blocks they used in the second row on the chart.

3. Say: *Next put the groups of blocks together to find the sum.* **Ask:** *Do you need to regroup? Do you have 10 units to exchange for a rod? Do you have 10 rods to exchange for a flat?* **Say:** *Now draw the new blocks you have all together on the chart.*

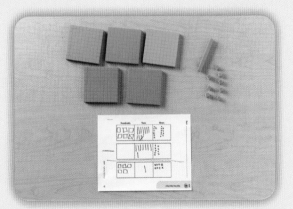

4. Say: *Take the sum from the first two numbers and draw it on the second chart. Now you need to subtract 89. Place a minus sign under the first row. Draw the blocks you have to subtract in the second row. Guide children in exchanging blocks to regroup and subtract.*

Use Base Ten Blocks. Build the numbers.
Find the sum or difference. (Check students' work.)

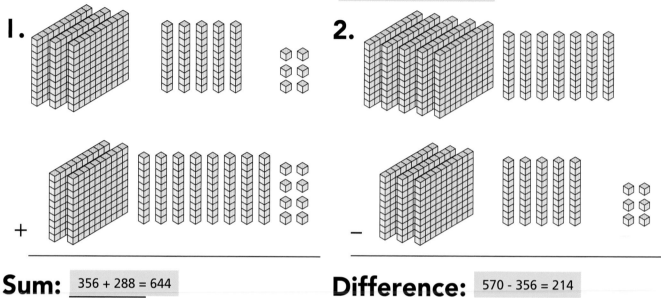

1.

2.

+

−

Sum: 356 + 288 = 644

Difference: 570 - 356 = 214

Use Base Ten Blocks. Build each number and draw the blocks. Find the sum or difference.

3. 489
     + 246

4. 638
     − 157

735

481

Find each sum or difference.

5. 335 − 254 = ___81___

6. 316 + 278 = ___594___

Download student pages at hand2mind.com/hosstudent.

Challenge! Leah built the number 568 with Base Ten Blocks. She gave some of these blocks to her friend. Then she had 350 blocks left. How many blocks did she give away? Use drawings or numbers to show your answer.

Challenge: 218; drawing should show 568 in blocks with 350 crossed out; number sentence 568 – 350 = 218.

Objective

Add 10 or 100.

Common Core State Standards

- **2.NBT.8** Mentally add 10 or 100 to a given number 100–900, and mentally subtract 10 or 100 from a given number 100–900.

Number and Operations in Base Ten

Adding 10 or 100

With a thorough understanding of place value, children can use mental math to add 10 or 100 to a given number. With practice, children realize that adding 10 affects the tens place and adding 100 affects the hundreds place without changing the ones place. They know also that if 10 is added to 190, 290, 390, 490, 590, 690, 790, or 890, then the hundreds place is affected. Manipulatives such as Base Ten Blocks can help children understand the place value changes involved in adding 10 or 100.

Try It! *Perform the Try It! activity on the next page.*

Talk About It

Discuss the Try It! activity.

- Write *148 + 100* in vertical format on the board. **Ask:** *Do we need to change the ones? Do we need to change the tens? Do we need to change the hundreds?* **Say:** *When we add 100, we only need to increase the hundreds by 1, since zeros are added in the tens and ones places.*

- Write *148 + 10* in vertical format on the board. **Ask:** *Do we need to change the ones? Do we need to change the tens? Do we need to change the hundreds?* **Say:** *When we add 10, we only need to increase the tens by 1, since zero is added in the ones place.*

- **Ask:** *Why would it be easy to add 10 or 100 in your head without writing the problem down?*

Solve It

With children, reread the problem. Have children write the number sentences that solve the parts of the problem. Then have them write a sentence telling why it is easy to add 10.

More Ideas

For other ways to teach adding 10 or 100—

- Have children pick 3 digits from a bag and create a three-digit number. Have them build the number with Base Ten Blocks. Next have children add 10 and then add 100 to the original number.

- Have children work in pairs. Have one child write a three-digit number. Have the second child build the number with Base Ten Blocks and add either 10 or 100 to the number. Have the first child decide if 10 or 100 were added and write the new number. Switch roles and repeat.

Formative Assessment

Have children try the following problem.

Which digit in 723 changes if 100 is added?

A. 2   **B.** 3   **C.** 7

Try It! 25 minutes | Pairs

Here is a problem about adding 10 or 100.

The gym teacher tracks how many sit-ups the children have done in class. So far, Giana has done 148 sit-ups. Her fiend Baillie has done 100 sit-ups. How many sit-ups have both girls done in all? How many sit-ups will each girl have if she does 10 more in the next class?

Introduce the problem. Then have children do the activity to solve the problem. Distribute Base Ten Blocks, paper, and pencils to children.

Materials

- Base Ten Blocks (5 flats, 10 rods, and 20 units per pair)
- paper (1 sheet per pair)
- pencils (1 per pair)

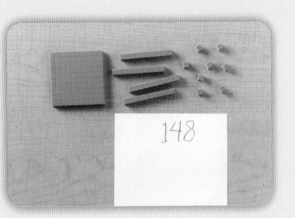

1. Say: *Let's use blocks to show the number of sit-ups Giana has done.* **Ask:** *How many hundreds do we need? How many tens do we need? How many ones do we need?*

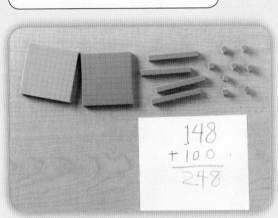

2. Say: *Now let's show how many sit-ups Baillie has done.* Have children model 100. **Say:** *Put the blocks together to add the numbers.* Write 148 + 100 in vertical format on the board. **Ask:** *When you combined the blocks, did you change the ones? Did you change the tens? Did you change the hundreds?* **Say:** *Write the sum on your paper.*

⚠ Look Out!

Watch for children who want to regroup every time they add 100. Explain that they only need to regroup if they have 10 or more rods or flats. Any other time, they just increase the tens or hundreds place without regrouping.

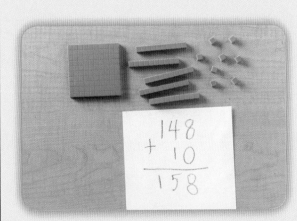

3. Say: *Let's find how many sit-ups each girl will have if she does 10 more in the next class.* **Ask:** *What do we need to add to each group of blocks? Does adding a ten change the ones? Does adding a ten change the hundreds?*

Look at the number. Then look at the blocks. Build the model. Decide if 10 or 100 were added. Write 10 or 100.

(Check students' work.)

1. $453 +$ ___10___

2. $387 +$ ___100___

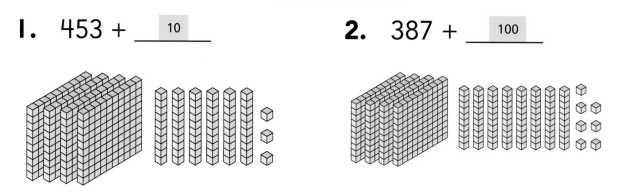

Look at the first number. Draw a model. Look at the sum. Decide if 10 or 100 need to be added. Write 10 or 100.

3. $264 +$ ___100___ $= 364$

4. $528 +$ ___100___ $= 628$

Look at each number. Add 10. Then add 100. Write both sums.

5.
$$489 \\ + \ 10 \\ \overline{499}$$

$$489 \\ + \ 100 \\ \overline{589}$$

6.
$$837 \\ + \ 10 \\ \overline{847}$$

$$837 \\ + \ 100 \\ \overline{937}$$

7.
$$648 \\ + \ 10 \\ \overline{658}$$

$$648 \\ + \ 100 \\ \overline{748}$$

8.
$$129 \\ + \ 10 \\ \overline{139}$$

$$129 \\ + \ 100 \\ \overline{229}$$

Download student pages at hand2mind.com/hosstudent.

Challenge! When we add 10 to a number, we usually only need to increase the tens by one. Is there a time when adding 10, that you need to change the number in the hundreds place? Use drawings or words to show your answer.

Challenge: (Sample) Yes; If I add 10 to 90, then I have to add 1 to the hundreds and make the tens a zero.

© ETA hand2mind™

Subtracting 10 or 100

Objective

Subtract 10 or 100.

Common Core State Standards

- **2.NBT.8** Mentally add 10 or 100 to a given number 100–900, and mentally subtract 10 or 100 from a given number 100–900.

With a thorough understanding of place value, children can use mental math to subtract 10 or 100 from a given number. With practice, children realize that subtracting 10 affects the tens place and subtracting 100 affects the hundreds place without changing the ones place. They know also that if 10 is subtracted from 100, 200, 300, 400, 500, 600, 700, 800, or 900, then the hundreds place is affected. Manipulatives such as Base Ten Blocks can help children understand the place value changes involved in subtracting 10 or 100.

Try It! Perform the Try It! activity on the next page.

Talk About It

Discuss the Try It! activity.

- Write *327 – 10* in vertical format on the board. **Ask:** *When we subtract, do we need to change the ones? Do we need to change the tens?* **Say:** *When we subtract 10, we decrease the tens by one. We do not change the ones, since zero is subtracted in the ones place.*

- Write *327 – 100* in vertical format on the board. **Ask:** *Do we need to change the ones? Do we need to change the tens? Do we need to change the hundreds?* **Say:** *We only need to change the hundreds, because zero is subtracted in the tens and ones places. We decrease the hundreds by 1.*

- **Ask:** *Why would it be easy to subtract 10 or 100 in your head without writing the problem down?*

Solve It

With children, reread the problem. Have children write the number sentences that solve the parts of the problem. Then have them write a sentence telling why it is easy to subtract 10 or 100.

More Ideas

For other ways to teach subtracting 10 or 100—

- Have children pick 3 digits from a bag and create a three-digit number. Have them build the number with Base Ten Blocks. Next have children subtract 10 and then subtract 100 from the original number.

- Have children work in pairs. Have one child write a three-digit number. Have the second child build the number with Base Ten Blocks and subtract either 10 or 100 from the number. Have the first child decide if 10 or 100 were subtracted and write the new number. Switch roles and repeat.

Formative Assessment

Have children try the following problem.

Which digit in 319 changes if 10 is subtracted?

A. 1   **B.** 3   **C.** 9

Try It! 25 minutes | Pairs

Here is a problem about subtracting 10 or 100.

The second grade classes collected canned goods for the local food bank. Mrs. Dell's class collected 327 canned goods. Mr. Larson's class collected 10 less than Mrs. Dell's class. Miss Johnson's class collected 100 less than Mrs. Dell's class. How many canned goods did Mr. Larson's and Miss Johnson's classes collect?

Introduce the problem. Then have children do the activity to solve the problem. Distribute Base Ten Blocks, paper, and pencils to children.

Materials
- Base Ten Blocks (10 flats, 10 rods, and 15 units per pair)
- paper (1 sheet per pair)
- pencils (1 per pair)

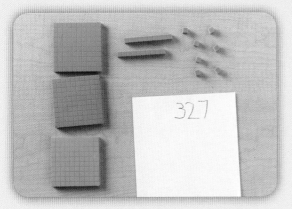

1. Say: *Let's use blocks to show the number of canned goods Mrs. Dell's class collected.* **Ask:** *How many hundreds do we need? How many tens do we need? How many ones do we need?*

2. Say: *Now let's find the number of canned goods Mr. Larson's class collected. They collected 10 less.* **Ask:** *Do we need to change the ones? Do we need to change the tens? Do we need to change the hundreds?* **Say:** *We subtract 1 ten from the 2 tens, to give us 1 ten. Write the difference on your paper.*

⚠ Look Out!

Watch for children who are not lining up their numbers correctly. If the place values aren't aligned, the children will not subtract properly and will not get the correct answer. If children repeatedly have difficulties, have them use grid or graph paper to keep their digits aligned

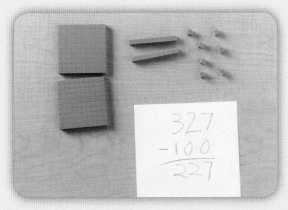

3. Say: *Let's find the number of canned goods Miss Johnson's class collected. They collected 100 less than Mrs. Dell's class.* **Ask:** *Do we need to change the ones? Do we need to change the tens? Do we need to change the hundreds?* **Say:** *We subtract 1 hundred from the 3 hundreds. Write the difference on your paper.*

Look at the number. Then look at the blocks. Build the model. Decide if 10 or 100 were subtracted. Write 10 or 100.

(Check students' work.)

1. $408 -$ [100]

2. $279 -$ [10]

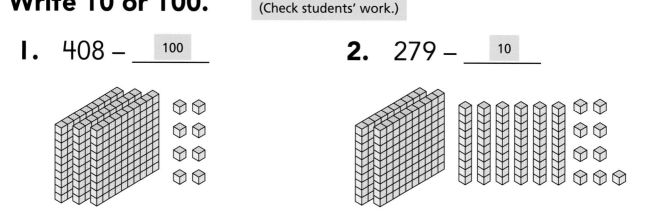

Look at the first number. Draw a model. Look at the difference. Decide if 10 or 100 need to be subtracted. Write 10 or 100.

3. $189 -$ [10] $= 179$

4. $528 -$ [100] $= 428$

Look at each number. Subtract 10. Then subtract 100. Write both differences.

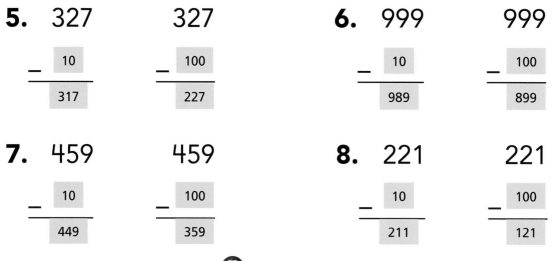

5. 327 327

$-$ [10] $-$ [100]

[317]   [227]

6. 999 999

$-$ [10] $-$ [100]

[989]   [899]

7. 459 459

$-$ [10] $-$ [100]

[449]   [359]

8. 221 221

$-$ [10] $-$ [100]

[211]   [121]

Challenge! When we subtract 10 from a number, we usually only need to decrease the tens by one. Is there a time when subtracting 10, that you need to change the number in the hundreds place? Use drawings or words to show your answer.

Challenge: (Sample) Yes; If I subtract 10 from 0 tens, then I will need to borrow from the hundreds and change the number in the hundreds place.

_____

_____

_____

_____

_____

_____

© ETA hand2mind™

Measurement and Data

In second grade, children build upon their nonstandard measurement experiences by measuring in standard units. They use *customary* (inches, feet, etc.) and *metric* (centimeters, meters, etc.) units to measure lengths of objects by selecting appropriate tools. They select an attribute to be measured, choose an appropriate unit of measurement, and determine the number of units.

In second grade, children also measure an object using two units of different lengths (e.g., a desk measured in inches and in feet). Doing so helps children realize that the unit used and the attribute being measured are both important. They estimate lengths using inches, feet, centimeters, and meters, which helps them become more familiar with unit sizes. Children make connections between number lines and rulers. They use length to solve addition and subtraction word problems and create number lines with equally spaced points corresponding to whole numbers to solve problems to 100.

Children extend skip-counting by 5s to tell and write time from analog and digital clocks to the nearest five minutes. Children solve word problems involving dollar bills, quarters, dimes, nickels, and pennies. They use measurement data as they pose questions, collect, analyze, and represent data, and interpret the results. They represent the lengths of several objects by making a line plot, where the horizontal scale is marked off in whole-number units. They draw picture graphs and bar graphs to represent data sets with up to four categories, and they solve simple problems using information presented in bar graphs.

The Grade 2 Common Core State Standards for Measurement and Data specify that children should—

- Measure and estimate lengths in standard units.
- Relate addition and subtraction to length.
- Work with time and money.
- Represent and interpret data.

The following hands-on activities provide children necessary experiences measuring, working with time and money, and representing and interpreting data. Using concrete materials prior to predicting, estimating, comparing, and solving problems enables children to acquire foundational concepts and gives them the confidence necessary to solve more difficult problems.

Measurement and Data

Contents

Objective

Estimate and measure length using standard units.

Common Core State Standards

- **2.MD.1** Measure the length of an object by selecting and using appropriate tools such as rulers, yardsticks, meter sticks, and measuring tapes.
- **2.MD.3** Estimate lengths using units of inches, feet, centimeters, and meters.

Measurement and Data

Standard Units

When children have had many opportunities to measure using nonstandard units, the transition to standard units is much easier. For less confusion, children should begin measuring in inches, using a ruler without smaller divisions. Estimating lengths can be difficult for children who have little experience measuring because it is hard for them to visualize. However, when children can use a benchmark to base their estimates, the process becomes less abstract.

Try It! Perform the Try It! activity on the next page.

Talk About It

Discuss the Try It! activity.

- **Ask:** *Did all your measurements come out pretty close?*
- **Say:** *Suppose some groups used Pattern Blocks, some used Snap Cubes®, and others used Inchworms™.* **Ask:** *Would the measurements come out just as close as when we all used Inchworms? Why or why not?*
- Discuss the importance of measuring using standard units. **Ask:** *Why might it be important that people all measure things using the same units?* Discuss what would happen if people did not have standard units with which to measure.

Solve It

With children, reread the problem. Have children write Dana a letter telling her how to find out which eraser is longer. Have children discuss using standard units or inches as units in their letters.

More Ideas

For other ways to teach about estimating and measuring length in standard units—

- Have pairs of children estimate the length of a desk in Color Tiles and Inchworms. Then have children measure the desk with both kinds of manipulatives, compare their estimates with the measurements, and compare the measurements.
- Have children use Snap Cubes and Inchworms to measure various classroom objects. Have them first estimate the lengths of the objects and then use the manipulatives to measure them. Have children compare their measurements using the different manipulatives. (Children should conclude that cubes are smaller units than Inchworms.)

Formative Assessment

Have children try the following problem.

How many Inchworms does this string measure?

A. 6 Inchworms **B.** 3 Inchworms **C.** 5 Inchworms

Try It! 30 Minutes | Groups of 3

Here is a problem about estimating and measuring lengths using standard units.

Dana's class is measuring things they find in the classroom. Dana tells her friend Steve that she thinks the board eraser in her room is longer than the eraser in his room. How can she find out if she is right?

Introduce the problem. Then have children do the activity to solve the problem.

Distribute Inchworms, paper, and crayons to children.

Materials
- Inchworms™ (12 per group)
- paper (1 sheet per child)
- crayons (1 per child)

1. Have children hold and carefully examine some Inchworms. **Ask:** *How many Inchworms long do you think the classroom eraser is?* Then have group members discuss their estimates.

2. Next have groups of children take turns using Inchworms to measure the classroom eraser. Have each group member write down his or her measurement.

3. Have children compare their estimates to their actual measurements. Then ask each group to tell their actual measurements. Have children clarify that Inchworms, or inches, are being used as units.

⚠ Look Out!

Children might not take care in lining up the Inchworms with the ends of the erasers. Make sure that the Inchworms reach the ends and that they are linked together. Guide children to see how not having the Inchworms or measurement tool aligned will cause inaccurate measurement.

Use Inchworms. Measure each item.

(Check students' work.)

1.

_____ 6 _____ inches

2.

_____ 8 _____ inches

Find each item. Estimate the length.
Use Inchworms to measure the length.

Answers will vary.

3. one side of a book

Estimate: _____ inches

Actual: _____ inches

4. straw

Estimate: _____ inches

Actual: _____ inches

5. crayon

Estimate: _____ inches

Actual: _____ inches

6. dollar

Estimate: _____ inches

Actual: _____ inches

Challenge! How is measuring with Inchworms like measuring with a ruler? How is it different?

Challenge: (Sample) An Inchworm is 1 inch long. Putting 12 Inchworms together end to end is the same as having a 12-inch ruler.

_____

_____

_____

_____

_____

_____

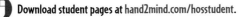
© ETA hand2mind™

Inches and Feet

As an important application of mathematics, measurement needs careful attention. Children must understand the need for standard units of measure and that inches and feet are customary units that are used in the United States. The relationship between inches and feet needs to be explored with children as they discover how many inches comprise one foot and how to measure the length of different objects.

Objective

Recognize the relationship between inches and feet.

Common Core State Standards

- **2.MD.1** Measure the length of an object by selecting and using appropriate tools such as rulers, yardsticks, meter sticks, and measuring tapes.
- **2.MD.3** Estimate lengths using units of inches, feet, centimeters, and meters.

Try It! *Perform the Try It! activity on the next page.*

Talk About It

Discuss the Try It! activity.

- **Ask:** *How long is one Inchworm?* Guide children to use the word *inch* to describe the length.
- **Say:** *One Inchworm is 1 inch long.* **Ask:** *How many inches long is the Inchworms™ Ruler?*
- **Say:** *The ruler is 12 inches long.* **Ask:** *What is another word for something that is 12 inches long?* Guide children to use the word *foot* to describe the length of the ruler.
- **Ask:** *How many inches long is your desk? Is your desk more than a foot long? How does this compare with your estimate?* Ask children to describe the length of their desk in feet and inches.

Solve It

With children, reread the problem. Have children act out the problem, using the measurements of their desks. Tell them that their desks must be at least 2 feet long for the model to fit on it. Have children figure out whether or not the model would fit.

More Ideas

For other ways to teach about the relationship between inches and feet—

- Children can trace their partner's body on butcher paper and then measure the tracing of their own body. First have them estimate their height to the nearest foot. Then have them draw one straight line from head to toe on the tracing and use an Inchworms Ruler to measure the length of the line.
- Have children use the Inchworms and Inchworms Ruler to measure other objects in the classroom. Ask them to make an estimate in inches or feet, measure, and compare estimates and actual measurements.

Formative Assessment

Have children try the following problem.

Which is the most likely measurement for the length of a baseball bat?

A. 6 inches **B.** 10 feet **C.** 3 feet

Try It! 30 minutes | Pairs

Here is a problem about recognizing the relationship between inches and feet.

Billy wants to bring his plane model for show-and-tell. He wants to put it on his desk, but he doesn't want anyone to walk into it and knock it down. He knows that his model is 2 feet long. How can Billy figure out if his model will fit on his desk?

Introduce the problem. Then have children do the activity to solve the problem.

Distribute 12 Inchworms and 1 Inchworms Ruler to each pair of children.

Materials
- Inchworms™ (12 per pair)
- Inchworms Ruler (1 per pair)

1. Ask children to compare the length of one Inchworm to the length of one Inchworms Ruler. Guide them to notice that one Inchworm is the same length as one numbered space on the Inchworms Ruler.

2. Have children explore how many Inchworms equal the length of the Inchworms Ruler. Ask children to make an Inchworms train that is the same length as the Inchworms Ruler. Then have them count the number of Inchworms used. Introduce *foot* as being equal to 12 inches.

3. Ask children to estimate the length of their desks using Inchworms. Ask children to measure the length of their desk or table using the Inchworms Ruler. They should first measure across from left to right. Then have children measure from bottom to top.

⚠ Look Out!

Children may not have a great deal of practice using rulers. Because of this, they may make errors while measuring. Remind children that they need to make sure that the zero mark of the Inchworms Ruler lines up with the end of the object. If an object is more than 12 inches long, emphasize that they must measure part and then move the Inchworms Ruler, being careful not to measure the same area twice. They can make a mark or put an object, such as a pencil point, at the end of the Inchworms Ruler to mark its place.

Use Inchworms and an Inchworms Ruler. Draw a line to match the measuring tool with the unit it measures. (Check students' work.)

1. inch

Check that students have drawn a line to the Inchworms.

2. foot

Check that students have drawn a line to the Inchworms Ruler.

Estimate the length of each. Use Inchworms and an Inchworms Ruler to measure each item in your class. Answers will vary.

3. width of door

Estimate   Actual

_____ feet   _____ feet

_____ inches   _____ inches

4. table

Estimate   Actual

_____ feet   _____ feet

_____ inches   _____ inches

© ETA hand2mind™

Challenge! Name something that is about 1 inch long. Name something that is about 1 foot long.

Challenge: Answers will vary.

Choosing a Unit

Choosing the appropriate unit requires children to use judgment in terms of the length of the object before they measure it. This judgment will improve as children gain experience with length. Another important part of cultivating judgment about units is exploring and understanding the relationship between units.

Objective

Choose the appropriate unit to measure length.

Common Core State Standards

■ **2.MD.1** Measure the length of an object by selecting and using appropriate tools such as rulers, yardsticks, meter sticks, and measuring tapes.

■ **2.MD.2** Measure the length of an object twice, using length units of different lengths for the two measurements; describe how the two measurements relate to the size of the unit chosen.

Try It! *Perform the Try It! activity on the next page.*

Talk About It

Discuss the Try It! activity.

■ **Ask:** *What units would you use to measure a classroom eraser? Why? What units would you use to measure a chair? Why?* Allow volunteers to measure both an eraser and a chair using the appropriate units.

■ **Say:** *You can often decide before you measure an object which units to use.* **Ask:** *Which units would you use to measure the height of the door?*

■ Ask children to think of examples of things at home or in school that they might measure using inches. Then have them think of things they might use feet to measure.

Solve It

With children, reread the problem. Have children identify the correct units for measuring the box for paper clips and the poster. Children may practice using Inchworms™ to measure a paper clip and the Inchworms Ruler to measure a piece of poster board. Then on one side they can make their own posters with drawings of things that can be measured with inches, and on the other side things that can be measured with feet.

More Ideas

For other ways to teach about choosing units to measure length—

■ Have children think of classroom objects that are best measured using a combination of both feet and inches. Then have groups use Inchworms and the Inchworms Ruler to take measurements and compare data for accuracy.

■ Ask children to compare the Inchworms Ruler to the lengths of their own feet. Have children see if real feet like theirs are 12 inches long like the measurement unit called *foot*. Children should conclude that their feet vary in size and are usually less than 12 inches, or 1 foot, long.

Formative Assessment

Have children try the following problem.

Which unit is best to measure your bed?

A. Inches   **B.** Feet   **C.** Snap Cubes®

Try It! 30 minutes | Pairs

Here is a problem about choosing the appropriate unit.

Bryan wants to see if he can fit paper clips into a small box. He also wants to find out if a rolled-up poster will fit in his desk. He needs to measure the length of both the paper clips and the poster to see if they will fit where he wants to put them. What units should he choose to measure these objects?

Introduce the problem. Then have children do the activity to solve the problem.

Distribute Inchworms, Inchworms Rulers, recording sheets, and pencils. Remind children that each Inchworm is 1 inch long and each Inchworms Ruler is 12 inches, or 1 foot, long.

Materials

- Inchworms™ (12 per pair)
- Inchworms Ruler (1 per pair)
- Measurement Recording Sheet 1 (BLM 9; 1 per pair)
- pencil, 6–8 inches long (1 per pair)

1. Have partners use one Inchworms piece to measure the length of the teacher's desk, turning the Inchworms piece from head to toe as they measure. Have one partner record their measurement in the first box on the recording sheet.

2. Have partners use the Inchworms Ruler to remeasure the desk. Have them record the measurement in feet on their recording sheet. When they have finished recording, **ask:** *When we measure a long object, is it better to use inches or feet?*

⚠ Look Out!

Children may have trouble choosing the appropriate unit. Remind children to consider whether the object they want to measure is less than or greater than a foot. If the object is less than a foot, they should use inches. If the object is greater than a foot, they may want to use feet or a combination of feet and inches.

3. Have children measure the pencil in inches and feet. **Ask:** *When we measure a short object, is it better to use inches or feet?*

Use Inchworms and an Inchworms Ruler.
Make each Inchworms train.

(Check students' work.)

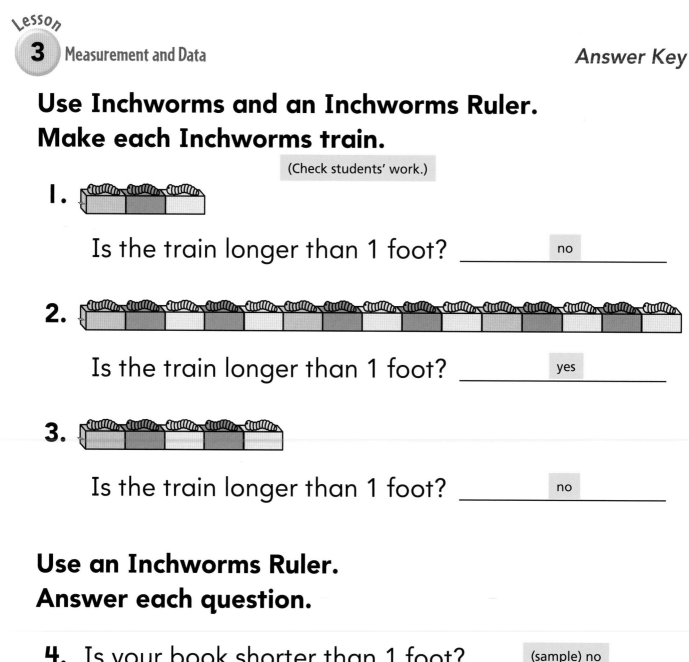

1. Is the train longer than 1 foot? _____ no

2. Is the train longer than 1 foot? _____ yes

3. Is the train longer than 1 foot? _____ no

Use an Inchworms Ruler.
Answer each question.

4. Is your book shorter than 1 foot?   (sample) no

5. Is your classroom wider than 1 foot?   yes

Which unit would you use to measure each item? Circle your answer.

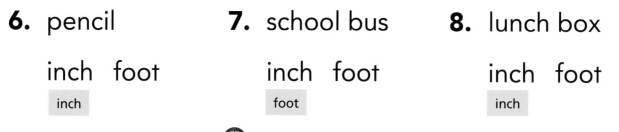

6. pencil

inch foot

inch

7. school bus

inch foot

foot

8. lunch box

inch foot

inch

© ETA hand2mind™

Challenge! A book is 12 Inchworms long.
Write its length two ways.

Challenge: (Sample) 12 inches and 1 foot

_____

_____

_____

_____

_____

_____

Estimating and Measuring

Measurement encompasses several areas of math. By this age, children will have experienced measuring objects with standard units. This exposure has formed a foundation of reference points that children can draw upon to make logical estimates and pick the best tools for measuring.

> **Try It!** *Perform the Try It! activity on the next page.*

Objective

Estimate and measure in customary and metric units.

Common Core State Standards

- **2.MD.3** Estimate lengths using units of inches, feet, centimeters, and meters.

Talk About It

Discuss the Try It! activity.

- **Ask:** *How many inches long did you estimate that the pencil would be? How many inches was it when you measured with Color Tiles?*

- **Ask:** *What was your estimate of the length of the pencil in centimeters? How many centimeters was it when you measured it with the unit cubes?*

- **Ask:** *How did you use the measurement of the pencil to help you estimate the length of the piece of paper? Did you use the measurements of the paper or pencil to help you estimate the length of the eraser? Why or why not?*

- Discuss with children the similarities and differences between inches and centimeters. Emphasize that inches and centimeters are both accurate ways to measure because they are both standard units.

Solve It

With children, reread the problem. Have children write a letter to Clyde explaining how he can measure in inches the same way he would measure using centimeters. They should tell Clyde how inches and centimeters are similar and different.

More Ideas

For other ways to teach about measuring in customary and metric units—

- Have children work in groups to trace outlines of their bodies on large sheets of paper and then measure from their feet to the top of their heads using both Color Tiles and Base Ten units.

- Have one child look around the room and select an object, estimating how long it is in inches or centimeters. Then have the child tell the class the estimate, using only the number and not the unit. The class then guesses the unit. Children then measure the object using Color Tiles and Base Ten units to find how close the estimate was.

Formative Assessment

Have children try the following problem.

Which is a good estimate of the length of your thumb?

A. 1 cm   **B.** 4 cm   **C.** 6 inches

Try It! 35 Minutes | Pairs

Here is a problem about measuring in customary and metric units.

Mr. Rossi asked his students to measure objects in inches. Clyde is a new student in Mr. Rossi's class. He is from England. He told Mr. Rossi that people use centimeters to measure in England. Mr. Rossi told Clyde to measure the objects with Centimeter Cubes while his partner measured with 1-inch Color Tiles. Who used more units to measure?

Introduce the problem. Then have children do the activity to solve the problem. Distribute Base Ten units, Color Tiles, recording sheets, pencils, and paper to children. Tell children that a tile is 1 inch long and a unit cube is 1 centimeter long. Explain that in the United States, we usually measure with customary units, such as inches and feet, but most other countries in the world use metric units, such as centimeters and meters.

Materials
- Base Ten Blocks (30 units per pair)
- Color Tiles (15 per pair)
- Measurement Recording Sheet 2 (BLM 10; 1 per pair)
- unsharpened pencil (1 per pair)
- $8\frac{1}{2}$" × 11" sheet of paper (1 per pair)

1. Have children estimate the length of the unsharpened pencil in tiles, then measure. Children should record the estimate and measurement on the recording sheet. They should then repeat the process with cubes.

2. Have children use their measurement of the pencil to estimate the length of a sheet of paper in inches. Children should measure with tiles and record the numbers. Have children repeat the activity for centimeters.

⚠ Look Out!

Some children may have trouble measuring accurately using cubes and tiles. Make sure children are lining up manipulatives correctly with the objects being measured. They should be careful not to leave gaps between the units of measure. Demonstrate for children that they will get a more accurate answer if the tiles and cubes are lined up correctly.

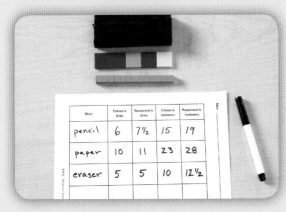

3. Have children repeat the steps of the activity to estimate and measure the length of a classroom eraser, and record their measurements.

Use Unit Cubes and Color Tiles to model the length of each item. Tell the length.

(Check students' work.)

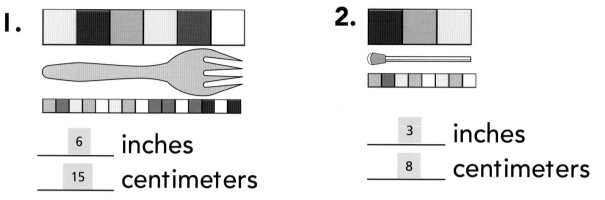

1. _____ 6 _____ inches
   _____ 15 _____ centimeters

2. _____ 3 _____ inches
   _____ 8 _____ centimeters

Using Unit Cubes and Color Tiles, model the length of each line. Tell the length.

3. ─────────────────

   _____ 4 _____ inches   _____ 10 _____ centimeters

4. ──────────────────────

   _____ 6 _____ inches   _____ 15 _____ centimeters

5. ─────────

   _____ 3 _____ inches   _____ 7 or 8 _____ centimeters

Find each item. Estimate its length.

For 6–8, answers will vary. Sample answers are given.

6. pencil
   _____ 6 _____ inches
   _____ 15 _____ centimeters

7. eraser
   _____ 1 _____ inch(es)
   _____ 3 _____ centimeters

8. paper clip
   _____ 2 _____ inches
   _____ 5 _____ centimeters

© ETA hand2mind™

Challenge!   When you measure the same object in inches and then centimeters, why is the number of centimeters always greater than the number of inches? Draw models of the units to help.

Challenge: (Sample) One inch equals about 2.5 centimeters. Because an inch is a longer distance, when a length is measured in both inches and centimeters, the number of inches will be a lesser number.

Objective

Measure differences in length.

Common Core State Standards

- **2.MD.4** Measure to determine how much longer one object is than another, expressing the length difference in terms of a standard length unit.

Measurement and Data

Comparing Two Lengths

Measuring and comparing the lengths of two different objects builds children's concept of size and helps prepare them to work with perimeter, area, and distance. In this activity, children will use Inchworms™ and the Inchworms Ruler to determine how many inches longer one object is than another. They will use their subtraction skills to find the difference.

Try It! Perform the Try It! activity on the next page.

Talk About It

Discuss the Try It! activity.

- **Ask:** *How long is the marker? How long is the crayon? How can Darlene find out how much longer the marker is than the crayon?* **Say:** *To find out how much longer one object is than another, we can measure both objects. Then we subtract the shorter length from the longer length.* **Ask:** *How much longer is the marker than the crayon?*

- **Say:** *When we compare the lengths of two objects, we must use the same unit of measurement for both objects. Let's say we compare two pieces of string and one piece is 1 foot long and the other piece is 9 inches long.* **Ask:** *Which piece is longer? How many inches are in a foot? How much longer is the string that is a foot, or 12 inches, than the one that is 9 inches?*

Solve It

With children, reread the problem. Have children measure each item with the Inchworms Ruler. Have them express their findings in a sentence, such as, "The marker is 2 inches longer than the crayon."

More Ideas

For other ways to teach about differences in length—

- Have pairs find five small objects around the room or in their desks to measure. Have one child pick two of the objects to compare. Have each child measure one of the objects using Inchworms and compare their measurements. Then have them complete the sentence: The _____ is _____ inches longer than the _____. Have children take turns picking two of the objects to measure.

- Have pairs use the Inchworms Ruler to measure two large objects in the room and compare the two lengths in feet.

Formative Assessment

Have children try the following problem.

How many inches longer is the bottom line than the top line?

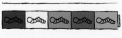

A. 2 inches   **B.** 3 inches   **C.** 4 inches

Try It! 25 minutes | Pairs

Here is a problem about finding the difference between the lengths of two objects.

Darlene knows that her markers are longer than her crayons, but she wants to know how much longer. How can she find out?

Introduce the problem. Then have children do the activity to solve the problem. Distribute Inchworms, Inchworms Rulers, markers, crayons, paper, and pencils to children.

Materials
- Inchworms™ (12 per pair)
- Inchworms Ruler (1 per pair)
- markers (1 per pair)
- crayons (1 per pair)
- paper (1 sheet per pair)
- pencils (1 per child)

1. Say: *First we need to measure the marker using the Inchworms and the ruler. Remember that Inchworms are an inch long, so our unit of measurement is inches.* **Ask:** *How many Inchworms, or inches, long is the marker?*

2. Say: *Now we need to measure the crayon. Place your crayon so that its flat end lines up with the left end of the marker and Inchworms.* **Ask:** *How many Inchworms, or inches, long is the crayon?*

⚠ Look Out!

Watch for children who aren't aligning the starting edges. It is easy for children to forget to keep things aligned. These children may benefit from having a book or notepad on the left to define the starting edge; children can place their items and Inchworms against it.

3. Say: *Now you can compare. You can count the number of Inchworms between the right end of the crayon and the right end of the marker. You also can subtract the length of the crayon from the length of the marker.* **Ask:** *How many inches longer is the marker than the crayon?*

Use Inchworms. Measure each item. Write how many inches longer one item is than the other.

(Check students' work.)

1.

___2___ inches longer

2.

___1___ inch(es) longer

3.

___4___ inches longer

Use an Inchworms Ruler. Measure the items. Answer the question.

Answers will vary.

4. How much longer is one side of a book than the other side?

one side ____ inches
other side ____ inches

_____ inches longer

5. How much longer is one side of your desk than the other side?

one side ____ inches
other side ____ inches

_____ inches longer

Download student pages at hand2mind.com/hosstudent.

Challenge! Draw two items from your room. Measure each item. Write the lengths. Write how much longer one item is than the other.

Challenge: Answers will vary. Check that children subtract correctly.

_____

_____

_____

_____

_____

_____

Objective

Represent whole numbers as lengths on a number line.

Common Core State Standards

■ **2.MD.6** Represent whole numbers as lengths from 0 on a number line diagram with equally spaced points corresponding to the numbers 0, 1, 2, ..., and represent whole-number sums and differences within 100 on a number line diagram.

Measurement and Data

Whole Numbers as Lengths on a Number Line

As children continue to become familiar with the units and processes of measuring length, they can begin to see a ruler as a number line and a number line as a ruler. By using rods of various lengths on a number line, they also can see units on the number line as whole numbers and whole numbers as lengths. Building trains of rods on a number line will help children understand how to add using a number line.

Try It! Perform the Try It! activity on the next page.

Talk About It

Discuss the Try It! activity.

■ **Say:** *Every space between ticks on the number line represents one.* **Ask:** *How many spaces do the 2 white rods cover?* **Say:** *So on this number line, one space equals the length of 1 white rod.*

■ **Ask:** *What is the value of the purple rod? Where did we place the purple rod on the number line? Starting at 2 and adding 4 using the purple rod, where do we end up?*

■ **Ask:** *What is the value of the dark green rod? Where did we place it on the number line? Starting at 6 and adding 6 using the dark green rod, where do we end up? What is the length of the train?*

■ **Ask:** *How is the number line like a ruler? How is it different?*

Solve It

With children, reread the problem. Have children draw the rods on the number lines. Have them write number sentences that represent the value of the train and its length.

More Ideas

For another way to teach about representing whole numbers as lengths—

■ For children who are having trouble, use 1-Inch Number Lines (BLM 12) and Inchworms™ to find various lengths of 1 through 8 inches. The larger unit and the ability to snap the Inchworms together might help children who are struggling.

Formative Assessment

Have children try the following problem.

How long is a train of 3 white rods, 2 red rods, and 1 light green rod on a centimeter number line?

A. 3   **B.** 7   **C.** 10

Try It! 25 minutes | Pairs

Here is a problem about representing whole numbers as lengths.

Ryan made a train of Cuisenaire Rods. He used 2 white rods, 1 purple rod, and 1 dark green rod. He built the train on a centimeter number line, starting at zero. At what number on the number line does the train end? What is the length of the train?

Introduce the problem. Then have children do the activity to solve the problem. Distribute Cuisenaire Rods, 1-cm Number Lines (BLM 11), crayons, paper, and pencils to children.

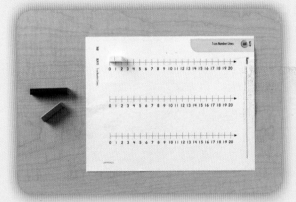

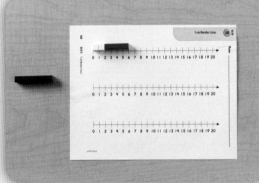

1. Ask: *Where should we start our train on the number line?* Remind children to start at zero and build the train to the right. **Ask:** *What is the value of the 2 white rods? What number does the second white rod end at?*

2. Say: *Now place the purple rod at the end of the white rods.* **Ask:** *How much more does the purple rod add? Where does the train end?* **Say:** *We can show this using a number sentence.* Write *2 + 4 = 6* on the board.

⚠ Look Out!

Watch for children who don't keep the train together. They might allow space between rods or allow the rods to move from zero. Explain that using a number line is like using a ruler. The left side of the train must align with 0.

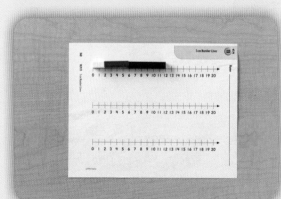

3. Say: *Now add the dark green rod at the end of the purple rod.* **Ask:** *How much does the dark green rod add to the train? Where does the train end? What is the length of the train?* **Say:** *You can show this using a number sentence, too.* Write *6 + 6 = 12*.

Use Cuisenaire Rods. Build the model. Write a number sentence for the lengths.

1.

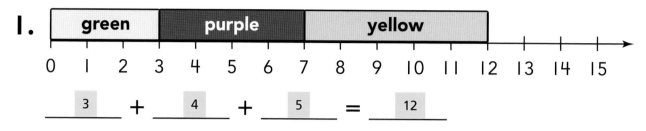

_____3_____ + _____4_____ + _____5_____ = _____12_____

Use two or three Cuisenaire Rods. Build the length. Draw the model. Write a number sentence.

2. 9 cm, two rods   (Check students' models.)

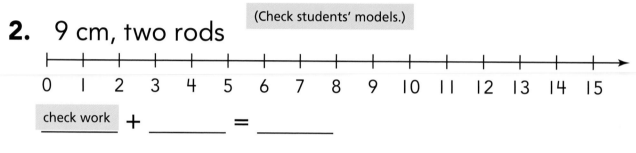

___check work___ + _____ = _____

3. 13 cm, three rods

___check work___ + _____ + _____ = _____

Show the total length on the number line.

4. 4 + 5 + 2 + 3 = ___14___

5. 3 + 3 + 5 + 2 = ___13___

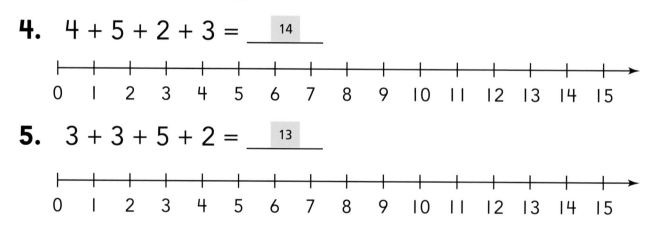

Download student pages at hand2mind.com/hosstudent.

Challenge! Nora and John are trying to find rods that would end at 19 on a number line. Nora says that 3 yellow rods and a purple rod would work. John says an orange and a blue rod would work. Who is correct, and why? Use words or drawings to explain.

Challenge: (Sample) Both are correct, because both total 19. Children may draw 2 number lines to show each set of rods. As long as both sets of rods are shown or described, it is correct.

© ETA hand2mind™

Time to 5 Minutes

Telling time is an important measurement skill that most young children are excited to learn. There are many real-life applications and repeated opportunities to reinforce this skill throughout the day. Making the most of these opportunities will give meaning to the concept of telling time and allow children to master the skill through repeated practice.

Objective

Tell time in 5-minute intervals before and after the hour.

Common Core State Standards

- **2.MD.7** Tell and write time from analog and digital clocks to the nearest five minutes, using a.m. and p.m.

Try It! *Perform the Try It! activity on the next page.*

Talk About It

Discuss the Try It! activity.

- Display a Geared Mini-Clock. **Say:** *The big numbers on a clock mark every 5 minutes when we look at the minute hand. The big numbers also mean hours when we look at the hour hand. Let's look how the minute hand moves as we count together by 5s.* Point to the small numbers on the clock as you count together from 5 to 60.

- **Ask:** *If the minute hand is pointing to the 4, how many minutes after the hour is it? What if the minute hand is pointing to the 7?*

- **Ask:** *If the time is 6:15, what number is the minute hand pointing to? If it is 45 minutes after the hour, what number is the minute hand pointing to?*

Solve It

With children, reread the problem. Then have children draw clocks to show 11:25 A.M. **Say:** *Dominic's class has to be in art class 5 minutes later. Draw another clock that shows what the time will be then.*

More Ideas

For other ways to teach about telling time to 5 minutes—

- Use Geared Mini-Clocks to display important times each morning. Ask volunteers to set one clock for music time, lunch, math, clean-up time, and so on. Display the clocks in a visible place in the room. Ask volunteers to write the event and the time on a sentence strip or construction paper to display with the clocks.

- Have children use Snap Cubes® to make 12 trains of 5 cubes. Use these to practice counting by 5s to 60.

Formative Assessment

Have children try the following problem.

Circle the time that the clock shows.

A. 5:35 P.M.

B. 7:25 P.M.

C. 7:45 P.M.

Try It! 20 minutes | Groups of 4

Here is a problem about telling time to 5 minutes.

Mr. Welch is reading a story to the class before they go to art. He asked Dominic to tell him when it is 11:25 A.M. so he can stop reading. How will Dominic know when it is 11:25 A.M. so the class is not late for art?

Introduce the problem. Then have children do the activity to solve the problem.

Distribute Geared Mini-Clocks, recording sheets, and pencils to children. **Say:** *The clocks have big red numbers and small blue numbers. Between the numbers are dots.* Start with the minute hand on the 12. Move the hand along the blue minute dots one by one and have the class count together. Stop at 5, write the time on the board, and discuss. **Ask:** *What do the dots stand for?*

Materials
- Geared Mini-Clock (1 per group)
- 5 Minutes Recording Sheet (BLM 13; 1 per child)
- pencils (1 per child)

1. Say: *Joshua woke up at 7:10 A.M.* Have children work together to model the time on their clocks.

2. Instruct children to draw the clock hands on Clock 1 on their 5 Minutes Recording Sheets and record the time.

3. Say: *Miss Green's class eats lunch at 12:25 P.M. each day.* Have children show this time on the clock and draw the hands on Clock 2. **Say:** *Use skip-counting to find how many minutes after 12 this is.* Repeat using other scenarios for Clocks 3 and 4.

⚠ Look Out!

Children may believe that 7:10 means the minute hand is on the big red 10. Reinforce the fact that children must count by 5s (or observe the small blue numbers) to find the correct placement for the minute hand. Remind children that the large numbers on the clock mark the hours, not the minutes.

Use a Geared Clock. Model the time shown. Write the time.

(Check students' work.)

1.

2.

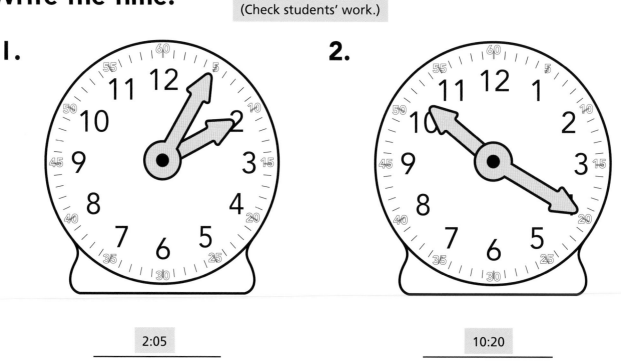

2:05

10:20

Use a Geared Clock. Model each time. Draw the hands on the clock.

3. 3:15

4. 7:40

Download student pages at hand2mind.com/hosstudent.

© ETA hand2mind™

Challenge! When the minute hand points to an hour number on the clock face, how do you know the number of minutes the time is?

Challenge: (Sample) Multiply that number by 5.

_____

_____

_____

_____

_____

_____

Know the relationship between the penny and the nickel.

- **2.MD.8** Solve word problems involving dollar bills, quarters, dimes, nickels, and pennies, using $ and ¢ symbols appropriately. *Example: If you have 2 dimes and 3 pennies, how many cents do you have?*

Measurement and Data

The Penny and Nickel

An understanding of money is an important life skill, as it is essential in paying for goods and services, making change, and checking that correct change has been received. Coin Tiles can help children visualize the relationships between coins and help children build a foundation for deeper work with money, such as performing operations with money amounts.

Try It! Perform the Try It! activity on the next page.

Talk About It

Discuss the Try It! activity.

- **Ask:** *How much does the toy car cost? How much money does Jared have? Which is greater, 22 or 20? Does Jared have enough money? How much more money does Jared need?*

- **Say:** *Place the 3 nickel tiles and the 5 penny tiles on the Hundred Board starting at 1.* **Ask:** *How many pennies would you need to reach 22?* On the board, write *22 – 20 = 2.*

- **Say:** *Let's say Jared's grandma gives him another nickel.* **Ask:** *How much money would he have? Would he have enough money to buy the toy car?* Have children put another nickel tile with their Coin Tiles and count the coins, or add 20 + 5.

Solve It

With children, reread the problem. Have children draw the coins and write a number sentence showing how much money Jared has. Have them write a sentence telling whether or not Jared can buy the car.

More Ideas

For other ways to teach about the relationship between pennies and nickels—

- Have children work in pairs. Have one child pick a handful of penny tiles out of a bag. Have that child trade in as many pennies as possible for nickels and give the coins to the other child. Have the second child place the tiles on a Hundred Board and tell how much money it is. Switch roles.

- Have children work in pairs. Have one child roll a number cube and take that many nickel tiles. Have the other child roll the number cube and take that many penny tiles. Have the two work together to add the values of the coins.

Formative Assessment

Have children try the following problem.

How many nickels equal 30 pennies?

A. 4   **B.** 5   **C.** 6

Try It! *30 minutes | Pairs*

Here is a problem about the relationship between pennies and nickels.

Jared wants to buy a toy car that costs 22 cents. He has 3 nickels and 5 pennies. Does he have enough money to buy the toy car?

Introduce the problem. Then have children do the activity to solve the problem. Distribute Coin Tiles, Hundred Boards, paper, pencils, and crayons to children.

Materials
- Coin Tiles (1 set per pair)
- Hundred Boards (1 per pair)
- paper (1 sheet per pair)
- pencils (1 per child)
- crayons (1 set per pair)

1. Ask: *What do we know about pennies and nickels? How much is 1 penny worth? How much is 1 nickel worth? How many pennies are worth 1 nickel?* **Say:** *Show how many pennies equal 1 nickel by placing penny tiles next to a nickel tile.*

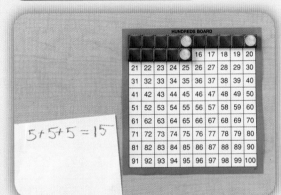

2. Say: *Jared has 3 nickels. We know that 1 nickel equals 5 pennies, or 5 cents.* **Ask:** *How much are 3 nickels worth?* Have children lay out 3 nickel tiles and count by 5s, or place the tiles on the Hundred Board to demonstrate the value. Have children write $5 + 5 + 5 = 15$. Then have them practice making the cent sign and write 15¢.

⚠ Look Out!

Watch for children who have difficulty knowing where to start placing tiles on the Hundred Board or how to position the tiles. Explain that they should start at 1 and build their amounts horizontally without skipping any spaces.

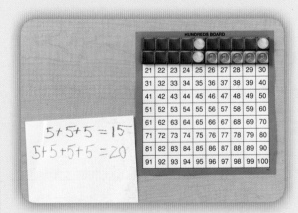

3. Ask: *How many pennies does Jared have?* **Say:** *Put 5 penny tiles with your 3 nickel tiles.* **Ask:** *How much are the 3 nickels worth? How much is 15 cents plus 5 cents? Does Jared have enough money to buy the toy car?*

Use Coin Tiles and a Hundred Board. Build the model. Write the total amount of money.

(Check students' work.)

1.

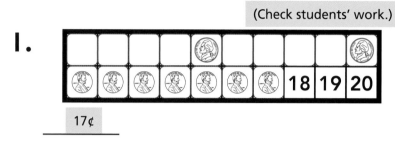

18 19 20

17¢

Use Coin Tiles and a Hundred Board. Build a model. Draw the model. Write the total amount of money.

2.

1	2	3	4	5	6	7	8	9	10
11	12	13	14	15	16	17	18	19	20
21	22	23	24	25	26	27	28	29	30

22¢

3.

1	2	3	4	5	6	7	8	9	10
11	12	13	14	15	16	17	18	19	20
21	22	23	24	25	26	27	28	29	30

25¢

Use Coin Tiles. Show the amount two ways using nickels and pennies. Draw the coins using red for nickels and purple for pennies.

4. 16¢

3 nickels and 1 penny,
2 nickels and 6 pennies,
1 nickel and 11 pennies

5. 25¢

4 nickels and 5 pennies,
3 nickels and 10 pennies,
2 nickels and 15 pennies,
1 nickel and 20 pennies

© ETA hand2mind™

Challenge! Thad has money for games at the fair. He has 27¢ in pennies. He wants to play at least 10 games of penny toss and some nickel races. How many nickel races can he play and keep at least 10¢ for penny toss? Draw or use words to explain.

Challenge: (Sample) He could use 3 nickels for the nickel race and have 12 pennies for the penny toss.

Measurement and Data

Penny, Nickel, and Dime

With an understanding of the penny and the nickel and the relationship between them, children expand their work with money to include the dime. They perform counting, exchanging, and adding operations with all three coins. Coin Tiles can help children visualize these operations.

Try It! *Perform the Try It! activity on the next page.*

Talk About It

Discuss the Try It! activity.

- **Ask:** *How many pennies equal a dime? How many dime tiles do we have on the Hundred Board?* On the board, write *10 + 10 + 10 + 10 = 40.*

- **Ask:** *How many pennies equal a nickel? How many nickel tiles do we have on the Hundred Board?* On the board, write *40 + 5 = 45.*

- **Ask:** *How many penny tiles do we have on the Hundred Board? Can you trade 3 pennies in for any other coin?* On the board, write *45 + 3 = 48¢.*

Solve It

With children, reread the problem. Have children use dime, nickel, and penny tiles to find a different way to make 48¢, and draw the coins that Chelsea can trade her pennies for. Have children write the value of the coins as a number sentence.

More Ideas

For other ways to teach about the relationships between pennies, nickels, and dimes—

- Give pairs an assortment of Coin Tiles. Have one child take the penny tiles and trade as many as possible for nickel tiles. Have the other child take the remaining nickel tiles and trade as many as possible for dime tiles. Have the pair determine the combined value of their tiles.

- Have pairs number a Four-Section Spinner (BLM 14) 1–4. Have them spin it three times to determine the numbers of penny, nickel, and dime Coin Tiles to take from a pile. Then have children place the tiles on a Hundred Board and tell how much money they have. Have them write a number sentence to represent the coins.

Formative Assessment

Have children try the following problem.

How many dimes can be traded for 6 nickels?

A. 2   **B.** 3   **C.** 12

Try It! 30 minutes | Pairs

Here is a problem about the relationships between pennies, nickels, and dimes.

Chelsea emptied her coin bank and sorted the coins. She had 48 pennies. She wants to exchange the pennies for nickels and dimes so she will have fewer coins. How many pennies will she have after the trade? If she wants the least possible number of coins, how many nickels and dimes will she get in the trade?

Introduce the problem. Then have children do the activity to solve the problem. Distribute Coin Tiles, Hundred Boards, paper, pencils, and crayons to children.

Materials
- Coin Tiles (1 set per pair)
- Hundred Boards (1 per pair)
- paper (1 sheet per pair)
- pencils (1 per child)
- crayons (1 set per pair)

1. Say: *We know that there are 5 pennies in 1 nickel.* **Ask:** *How much is 1 dime worth?* **Say:** *Show how many pennies equal 1 dime by placing penny tiles next to a dime tile. Show how many nickels equal 1 dime by placing nickel tiles next to a dime tile.*

2. Say: *Chelsea wants to trade 48 pennies for nickels and dimes. Find 48 on the Hundred Board. Pretend that each square is a penny.* **Ask:** *How many pennies can Chelsea trade for a dime?* **Say:** *Take 1 dime tile and place it over 10 pennies. Repeat this until you don't have enough pennies to trade for another dime.*

⚠ Look Out!

Watch for children who are struggling with seeing the type of coin that pennies can be traded for. Explain that trading for the greatest coins possible makes carrying and counting the coins easier. Remind them that each row on the Hundred Board is worth 10 cents and that counting dimes is like counting by tens.

3. Ask: *How many pennies are left? Can you trade any pennies for a nickel?* **Say:** *Place a nickel tile and penny tiles on the spaces that are left.* **Ask:** *How many pennies, nickels, and dimes can Chelsea trade her 48 pennies for?*

Use Coin Tiles and a Hundred Board. Build the model. Circle the coins you can trade for.

(Check students' work.)

1. 35 pennies

3 dimes, 1 nickel

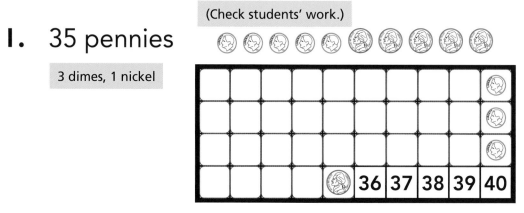

Use Coin Tiles and a Hundred Board. Build a model. Draw the model. Circle the coins you can trade for.

2. 3 nickels and 12 pennies   2 dimes, 1 nickel

1	2	3	4	5	6	7	8	9	10
11	12	13	14	15	16	17	18	19	20
21	22	23	24	25	26	27	28	29	30

Circle the coins you would use to pay for the item.

3. an apple that costs 34¢

3 dimes and 4 pennies, or 2 dimes, 2 nickels, and 4 pennies

4. a cookie that costs 27¢

2 dimes, 1 nickel, and 2 pennies

Write the total amount.

5.

_____ = 32¢ ¢

6.

 _____ = 26¢ ¢

Challenge! Hoda has 8 coins that equal 43 cents. She has 3 pennies. What are her other coins? Use the Hundred Board and Coin Tiles. Draw or write the 8 coins she has.

Challenge: 3 dimes, 2 nickels, and 3 pennies

_____

_____

_____

_____

_____

_____

Objective

Know the quarter.

Common Core State Standards

■ **2.MD.8** Solve word problems involving dollar bills, quarters, dimes, nickels, and pennies, using $ and ¢ symbols appropriately. *Example: If you have 2 dimes and 3 pennies, how many cents do you have?*

Understanding Quarters

When they're ready, children will relate their knowledge of the penny, nickel, and dime to the quarter. Since there are various coin combinations that are equivalent to a quarter, children will need to have a good understanding of the previous coins before advancing to the quarter. With the quarter being $\frac{1}{4}$, or 0.25, of a dollar, children will be able to carry their understanding of quarters into their study of fractions and decimals.

Try It! *Perform the Try It! activity on the next page.*

Talk About It

Discuss the Try It! activity.

■ **Ask:** *How many spaces do the 3 quarter tiles cover on the Hundred Board? How much are 3 quarters worth? Where should you place the 4 dime tiles? How many rows do the 4 dimes cover?* **Say:** *Now you need to decide how many nickels you can trade for the amount that is left.*

■ **Ask:** *How much of the 75¢ is left? How many nickels can be traded for 35 cents?* **Say:** *Place 7 nickel tiles on the remaining quarter tiles.* **Ask:** *Is there any part of the 75¢ left?* **Say:** *Sophie should give the boy 4 dimes and 7 nickels for his 3 quarters.*

Solve It

With children, reread the problem. **Ask:** *What if the boy asked for 3 dimes and the rest nickels? How many dimes and nickels would Sophie give the boy?* Have children use Coin Tiles on the Hundred Board to show the change and write or draw the number of dimes and nickels.

More Ideas

For other ways to teach about quarters—

■ Have pairs use the Four-Section Spinner (BLM 14) and draw a penny (purple circle), a nickel (red circle), a dime (blue circle), and a quarter (green circle) in the 4 sections. Have one child spin 4 times and show the coins with tiles on the Hundred Board. Have the second child tell the amount of the coins and tell another way to show the same amount. Switch roles and repeat.

■ Have partners pick a number (25¢–99¢) from a bag. Have one child show that amount using penny, nickel, and dime tiles. Have the other child show the amount using penny, nickel, dime, and quarter tiles. Switch roles and repeat.

Formative Assessment

Have children try the following problem.

Which coins equal 2 quarters?

A. 2 dimes, 2 nickels, 10 pennies   B. 3 dimes, 1 nickel, 10 pennies

C. 3 dimes, 2 nickels, 10 pennies

Try It! 30 minutes | Pairs

Here is a problem about understanding quarters.

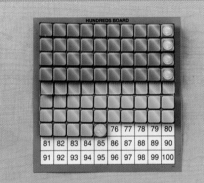

Sophie was helping make change at the school fair. Children were using coins to play the games. Different games cost different amounts. Many of the children came with quarters and wanted change for the nickel and dime games. One boy gave Sophie 3 quarters and asked for 4 dimes and the rest nickels. How many dimes and nickels should Sophie give the boy?

Introduce the problem. Then have children do the activity to solve the problem. Distribute Coin Tiles, Hundred Boards, paper, pencils, and crayons to children.

Materials
- Coin Tiles (1 set per pair)
- Hundred Boards (1 per pair)
- paper (1 sheet per pair)
- pencils (1 per child)
- crayons (1 set per pair)

1. Ask: *How much is a quarter worth?* Have children place dime, nickel, and penny tiles on top of a quarter tile to explore which coins equal a quarter. **Say:** *Since the boy gave Sophie 3 quarters, place 3 quarter tiles on the Hundred Board.* **Ask:** *How much are 3 quarters worth?*

2. Ask: *How many dimes did the boy ask for?* **Say:** *Use 4 dime tiles to cover part of the quarters on the Hundred Board.*

⚠ Look Out!

Watch for children who are having difficulty trading coins for quarters. Since a quarter's value does not end in 0, this may be confusing for some children. Provide these children more time to place dime, nickel, and penny tiles on top of the quarter tiles.

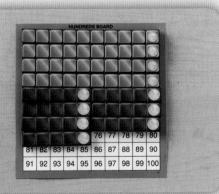

3. Ask: *How much is left of the 75 cents we started with? How many nickels can you make with the amount left?* **Say:** *Place nickel tiles on the remaining spaces to cover a total of 75 cents.*

Use Coin Tiles and a Hundred Board.
Find the value of the coins. (Check students' work.)

1.

= ___60¢___

2.

= ___48¢___

3.

= ___69¢___

4.

= ___96¢___

Draw the coins you would use to pay for the item.

5. a puzzle that
   costs 67¢

Possible answer:
2 quarters, 1 dime,
1 nickel, 2 pennies

6. a comic book that
   costs 88¢

Possible answer:
3 quarters, 1 dime,
3 pennies

Download student pages at hand2mind.com/hosstudent.

Challenge!   Josh has 6 coins in his pocket.
The coins total 56¢. Draw the coins that are
in his pocket.

Challenge: 1 quarter, 2 dimes, 2 nickels, and 1 penny

_____

_____

_____

_____

_____

Solve Problems Involving Coins

An understanding of the relationships between pennies, nickels, dimes, and quarters is essential to solving problems involving coins, such as the problems that children will encounter in real life. Practice with Coin Tiles can help children build confidence in handling money. And with sufficient confidence, children will be able to use mental math to find solutions to problems involving coins.

Objective

Solve problems involving pennies, nickels, dimes, and quarters.

Common Core State Standards

- **2.MD.8** Solve word problems involving dollar bills, quarters, dimes, nickels, and pennies, using $ and ¢ symbols appropriately. *Example: If you have 2 dimes and 3 pennies, how many cents do you have?*

Try It! *Perform the Try It! activity on the next page.*

Talk About It

Discuss the Try It! activity.

- **Ask:** *How much money did Jextin pay with? How can you find the total without using the Hundred Board? How much are 2 quarters worth? 4 dimes?* **Say:** *We can write this as 50 + 40 = 90¢.*

- **Ask:** *How much did the card cost? How much change did Jextin get?*

- **Say:** *When you find change, you are finding the difference between what is paid and the cost. You can "count up" from the cost to the amount paid to find the change. Jextin paid 90¢, and his card cost 83¢. To find his change, you count up from 83 to 90: 84, 85, 86, 87, 88, 89, 90. Since you counted out 7 ones, or pennies, the change is 7¢.*

- **Say:** *We also can find the amount of change by subtracting.* **Ask:** *How much is 90 minus 83? What coins can you use to make 7¢ change?*

Solve It

With children, reread the problem. Have children draw the coins Jextin started with and write the total amount. Then have them draw and write how much change Jextin received.

More Ideas

For another way to teach solving problems involving pennies, nickels, dimes, and quarters—

- Have pairs use Coin Tiles with the blank side of the Hundred Board. One child places Coin Tiles on the board. The other tells how many cents there are. The first child checks his/her partner's answer. Partners can double-check by placing the same Coin Tiles on the other side of the Hundred Board.

Formative Assessment

Have children try the following problem.

If you have 2 quarters, 2 dimes, 2 nickels, and 2 pennies, how much money do you have?

A. 72¢   **B.** 82¢   **C.** 87¢

Try It! 30 minutes | Pairs

Here is a problem involving pennies, nickels, dimes, and quarters.

Jextin went to the card store. He found a card that cost 83¢. He paid for the card using 2 quarters and 4 dimes. How much change did Jextin receive?

Introduce the problem. Then have children do the activity to solve the problem. Distribute Coin Tiles, Hundred Boards, paper, pencils, crayons, and markers to children.

Materials
- Coin Tiles (1 set per pair)
- Hundred Boards (1 per pair)
- paper (1 sheet per pair)
- pencils (1 per child)
- crayons (1 set per pair)
- dry erase markers (1 set per pair)

1. Say: *First let's put all the coins Jextin paid with on the Hundred Board. Start with the quarters, then add the dimes.* **Ask:** *How much money did Jextin pay?* Have children remove the tiles and circle 90 using a red crayon or dry erase marker.

2. Ask: *How much did Jextin's card cost?* Have children circle 83 on the Hundred Board using a blue crayon or dry erase marker.

⚠ Look Out!

Watch for children who don't count the number of squares past the cost of the card. Remind them that the change is the extra that was paid, which is represented on the Hundred Board by the distance from the cost to the amount paid.

3. Say: *The change Jextin received is the difference between the amount he paid and the cost. You need to count from the cost, 83¢, to the amount Jextin paid, 90¢. This is called "counting up." Find out how much change Jextin received.*

Answer Key

Use Coin Tiles and a Hundred Board. (Check students' work.)

1. Devin and Kevin want to buy a gift for their dad. Devin has 3 dimes, 1 nickel, and 3 pennies. Kevin has 1 quarter, 1 dime, 3 nickels, and 4 pennies. How much do they have together for the gift?

   _38_ + _54_ = _92¢_

Circle the price. Color the amount paid. Find the change.

2. Price 57¢; amount paid 75¢.

   57 circled, 75 colored, change: 18¢

   change: _____¢

1	2	3	4	5	6	7	8	9	10
11	12	13	14	15	16	17	18	19	20
21	22	23	24	25	26	27	28	29	30
31	32	33	34	35	36	37	38	39	40
41	42	43	44	45	46	47	48	49	50
51	52	53	54	55	56	57	58	59	60
61	62	63	64	65	66	67	68	69	70
71	72	73	74	75	76	77	78	79	80
81	82	83	84	85	86	87	88	89	90
91	92	93	94	95	96	97	98	99	100

3. Price 72¢; amount paid 80¢.

   72 circled, 80 colored, change: 8¢

   change: _____¢

1	2	3	4	5	6	7	8	9	10
11	12	13	14	15	16	17	18	19	20
21	22	23	24	25	26	27	28	29	30
31	32	33	34	35	36	37	38	39	40
41	42	43	44	45	46	47	48	49	50
51	52	53	54	55	56	57	58	59	60
61	62	63	64	65	66	67	68	69	70
71	72	73	74	75	76	77	78	79	80
81	82	83	84	85	86	87	88	89	90
91	92	93	94	95	96	97	98	99	100

4. Write the change for each row.

Price	Paid	Change
55¢		20¢
63¢		7¢
94¢		1¢
33¢		17¢

Download student pages at hand2mind.com/hosstudent.

© ETA hand2mind™

Challenge!   Phillip has 2 dimes, 4 nickels, and 3 pennies. Lauren has 1 quarter, 1 nickel, and 9 pennies. How much does each person have? Who has more money?

Challenge: Phillip: 43¢, Lauren: 39¢; Phillip has more money than Lauren.

_____

_____

_____

_____

_____

_____

© ETA hand2mind™

Geometry

In second grade, children describe and analyze shapes. By creating and analyzing two- and three-dimensional shapes, children develop a foundation for understanding geometry concepts such as congruence, similarity, and symmetry, which are necessary for learning in later grades. At this level, children recognize and draw shapes having specified attributes, such as a given number of sides or angles, or equal faces. They identify and name triangles, quadrilaterals (squares, rectangles, and trapezoids), pentagons, hexagons, and cubes.

Children partition rectangles into rows and columns of same-size squares and count to find the total number of them. They answer questions, such as, "How many ways can a square be partitioned into fourths?" This standard is connected with using arrays to work on repeated addition (2.OA.4).

Children also partition circles and rectangles into two, three, or four equal shares (or regions), describe the shapes using the words *halves*, *thirds*, *half of*, *a third of*, etc., and describe the whole as two halves, three thirds, or four fourths. They also learn that equal shares of identical wholes do not need to have the same shape.

The Grade 2 Common Core State Standards for Geometry specify that children should—

- Reason with shapes and their attributes.

The following hands-on activities with manipulatives will help children grasp the geometry concepts presented at second grade. Mathematically proficient second graders accurately use definitions and language to construct viable arguments about mathematics. During discussions about geometry problems, children should be given opportunities to constructively critique strategies and reasoning with their classmates. Teachers will want to ensure there is ample time for children to communicate about shapes and their attributes.

Geometry

Contents

Objective

Identify characteristics of plane shapes.

Common Core State Standards

- **2.G.1** Recognize and draw shapes having specified attributes, such as a given number of angles or a given number of equal faces. Identify triangles, quadrilaterals, pentagons, hexagons, and cubes.

Geometry

Identify Plane Shapes

Gaining a beginning understanding of basic geometric shapes and terms offers children the opportunity to use a different type of mathematical thinking. Although geometric thinking is related to numerical thinking, becoming familiar with shapes and developing spatial reasoning skills will lay the foundation for understanding in math, science, art, and social studies.

Try It! *Perform the Try It! activity on the next page.*

Talk About It

Discuss the Try It! activity.

- Have children look at their Shape Recording Sheet (BLM 15). **Ask:** *How many corners does a square have? How many sides?* Repeat for triangles and rectangles.

- Have children compare and contrast two shapes. For example, **ask:** *How is a square the same as a rectangle? How is a square different from a rectangle?* Repeat with other shapes.

Solve It

With children, reread the problem. Then have children draw a picture consisting of only squares, rectangles, and triangles. Instruct children to label each shape in their drawing and describe each shape. For an added challenge, state how many of each shape children are to include.

More Ideas

For other ways to teach about plane shapes—

- Have children use Pattern Blocks to find real-life objects that have the same shape. Encourage children to record the real-life objects that are shaped like each Pattern Blocks shape.

- Give each child a set of Tangrams and have them solve shape riddles. For example, **say:** *I'm thinking of a shape with three sides and three corners.* **Ask:** *What shape is it?* (triangle)

Formative Assessment

Have children try the following problem.

I am a shape with four sides and four corners. All four of my sides are the same length. What shape could I be?

A. triangle

B. rectangle

C. square

Try It! 15 minutes | Pairs

Here is a problem that involves identifying plane shapes.

During story time, Brandon's teacher told the children to sit on the floor. The children were to form a shape that has three straight sides and three corners. How can Brandon and his classmates figure out what shape they are to sit in?

Introduce the problem. Then have children do the activity to solve the problem.

Distribute Geoboards, rubber bands, a Shape Recording Sheet (BLM 15), and pencils to children.

Materials
- Geoboard (1 per pair)
- rubber bands (4 per pair)
- Shape Recording Sheet (BLM 15; 1 per pair)
- pencils (1 per child)

1. Instruct children to use the rubber bands to make a shape that has four straight sides of equal length and four corners. Tell children to count how many units each side is to be sure they are equal. Guide children to identify the shape as a square. **Ask:** *Is this the shape that the children are to sit in?*

2. Have children write "square" on their recording sheet and record the number of sides and corners this shape has.

3. Repeat Steps 1 and 2 for a rectangle and a triangle. After each shape has been made, **ask:** *Is this the shape that the children are to sit in?*

⚠ Look Out!

Make sure that children understand the difference between a square and a rectangle. Both have four sides and four corners. Reinforce the fact that in squares all four sides are of equal length. In rectangles only the opposite sides are equal, but all four sides are not.

Use a Geoboard and rubber bands. Make each shape. Tell the number of sides and corners.

(Check students' work.)

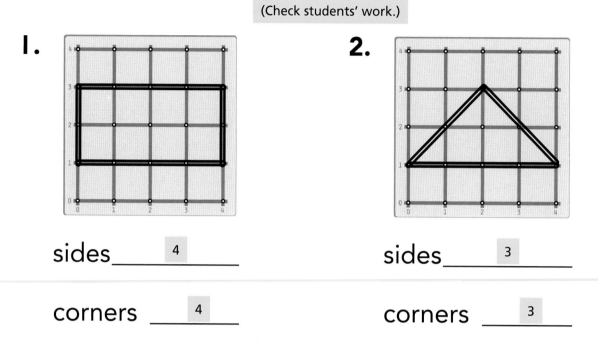

1.

sides _____4_____

corners _____4_____

2.

sides _____3_____

corners _____3_____

Use a Geoboard and rubber bands. Make each shape. Draw it. Tell the number of sides and corners.

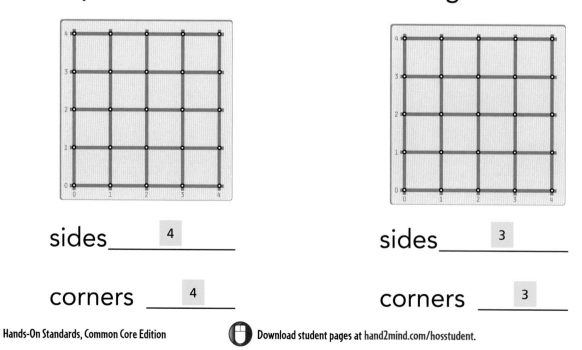

3. square

sides _____4_____

corners _____4_____

4. triangle

sides _____3_____

corners _____3_____

Download student pages at hand2mind.com/hosstudent.

© ETA hand2mind™

Challenge! Can a shape have more sides than corners? Explain your answer.

Challenge: (Sample) No; two sides meet to make each corner. Each side is used twice, so for every side, there is a corner.

_____

_____

_____

_____

_____

_____

© ETA hand2mind™

Building Cubes and Prisms

In grades 1 and 2, children become adept at exploring, describing, and representing the three-dimensional shapes in their environment. They explore three-dimensional shapes through composing and decomposing them, which augments their understanding of the nature of the shapes. Children need to see three-dimensional shapes in a variety of orientations and locations so that their understanding of the shapes encompasses real-life situations. Children also should make connections between two-dimensional shapes as they appear in three-dimensional solids.

Objective

Identify characteristics of cubes and rectangular prisms.

Common Core State Standards

■ **2.G.1** Recognize and draw shapes having specified attributes, such as a given number of angles or a given number of equal faces. Identify triangles, quadrilaterals, pentagons, hexagons, and cubes.

Try It! *Perform the Try It! activity on the next page.*

Talk About It

Discuss the Try It! activity.

■ Display the cubes. **Ask:** *What is this shape called? What do we know about all the faces on this shape?*

■ **Ask:** *How many faces does a cube have? How many edges and corners? What are some things you see every day that are shaped like cubes?*

■ Display two cubes to form a rectangular prism. **Ask:** *What shape do I have? How many faces, edges, and corners does it have? What are some things you see every day that are shaped like rectangular prisms?*

■ **Ask:** *What is an easy way to tell the difference between a cube and a rectangular prism?* (Cubes have faces that are all squares.) *What do you know about the number of faces, edges, and corners of these two shapes?* (Both shapes have the same number of faces—6, edges—12, and corners—8.)

Solve It

With children, reread the problem. Then have children write letters to Mrs. Talbot explaining how cubes and rectangular prisms are alike and different. Encourage children to use key words such as *faces, edges,* and *corners.*

More Ideas

For other ways to teach about rectangular prisms—

■ Have children use Snap Cubes® to create two larger cubes with the same dimensions (2 × 2 × 2). Then guide children to combine the two cubes to form a rectangular prism (4 × 2 × 2).

■ Have children use Color Tiles to create squares or rectangles in a two-dimensional array (2 × 2 or 2 × 3). Then have children use Snap Cubes and the dimensions of the tile arrays to create cubes and rectangular prisms having faces with the same dimensions.

Formative Assessment

Have children try the following problem.

How many edges does this figure have?

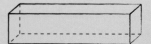

Try It! 20 minutes | Groups of 3

Here is a problem about cubes and rectangular prisms.

Mrs. Talbot has 20 boxes of books. Each box is square on all sides. Mrs. Talbot wants to arrange the boxes at the back of the room to make 2 large shapes. She builds a cube using 8 boxes. She builds a rectangular prism with 12 boxes. How many faces, edges, and corners does each shape have?

Introduce the problem. Then have children do the activity to solve the problem. Distribute the materials to children. Introduce and define the terms *face, edge,* and *corner.* Provide examples of each.

Materials
- 2-cm Color Cubes (20 per group)
- Cubes and Prisms Recording Sheet (BLM 16; 1 per child)
- pencils (1 per child)

1. Have children count the faces, edges, and corners on the cube. Establish that a cube is a shape that has square faces on all sides. Challenge children to use 8 cubes to make a large cube, like Mrs. Talbot did (2 × 2 × 2). Point out the faces, edges, and corners, making sure to concentrate on the attributes of the large cube formed, not each individual cube.

2. Guide children to build a rectangular prism measuring 1 × 1 × 2 using cubes. Discuss the differences between the rectangular prism and the cube shapes they built (concentrate on square faces versus rectangular faces on the two shapes). Challenge children to add the remaining cubes to the rectangular prism to make one that uses 12 cubes, like Mrs. Talbot did (3 × 2 × 2). Discuss the faces, edges, and corners on the large rectangular prism.

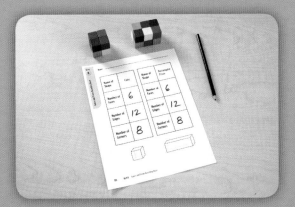

3. Have children complete the recording sheet while using their cube and rectangular prism models to guide them. Discuss the similarities and differences between the data and the way the two shapes look.

⚠ Look Out!

If children cannot count the number of faces (or edges or corners) correctly, ask them to touch each face (or edge or corner) as they count it. Reinforcing the number with a kinesthetic experience should help children count correctly. You might mark a face with tape to ensure it is not recounted. Also watch for children who count the edges of two faces separately, even when they are put together to form one edge.

Use 2-cm Color Cubes. Build each prism.
Tell the number of faces, edges, and corners.

(Check students' work.)

1.

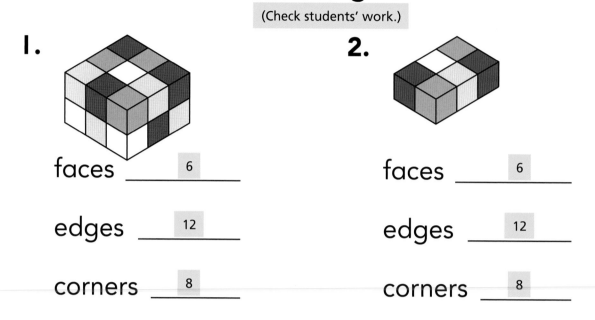

faces _____ 6

edges _____ 12

corners _____ 8

2.

faces _____ 6

edges _____ 12

corners _____ 8

Use 2-cm Color Cubes. Build each prism.
Draw the prism. Tell the number of faces,
edges, and corners.

3. 3 cubes long
3 cubes wide
3 cubes tall

4. 2 cubes long
4 cubes wide
3 cubes tall

faces _____ 6

edges_____ 12

corners _____ 8

faces _____ 6

edges_____ 12

corners _____ 8

Download student pages at hand2mind.com/hosstudent.

Challenge! Does a solid shape have more faces, corners, or edges? Is that always true?

Challenge: edges; yes

_____

_____

_____

_____

_____

Partitioning Rectangles

The concept of area ties together several strands of mathematics, including measurement, geometry, and number skills. As a transition to solving for area, children learn to partition rectangles into arrays of equal squares. This exposes them to the basic notion of area without the need for computation. Understanding attributes of rectangles and squares and having a sense of number will help children visualize area. Moreover, partitioning rectangles into arrays leads to the development of multiplication skills.

Try It! *Perform the Try It! activity on the next page.*

Talk About It

Discuss the Try It! activity.

- **Ask:** *What shape is the blanket? What do you know about rectangles? Why are there more rows than columns? How many rows are there? How many columns are there?*

- **Ask:** *How many color squares did you count in the rectangle?* Elicit that there are 8 rows of 5, and have children count the squares by 5s.

- **Ask:** *What if Maria and her grandmother decide the blanket is too small or too large? How many squares would there be if they added a row? Added a column? Subtracted a row? Subtracted a column?*

Solve It

With children, reread the problem. Have children draw the blanket with 8 rows of 5 squares. Have children count the total number of squares and write a sentence telling how many squares Maria and her grandmother need for the blanket.

More Ideas

For other ways to teach partitioning rectangles—

- Have pairs use Geoboards and the Four-Section Spinner (BLM 14) to create rectangles. Have them number the spinner 1–4 and spin twice for the number of squares across and the numbers of squares down for a rectangle. Have children partition the rectangle into rows and columns of squares and count how many squares there are in the rectangle.

- Have children use Geoboards to make various rectangles. Have them exchange boards with a partner and partition the rectangle into as many rows and columns of squares as they can. Then have them count to tell how many squares.

Formative Assessment

Have children try the following problem.

How many small squares are in this rectangle?

A. 18   B. 12   C. 9

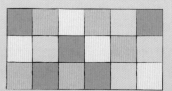

Objective

Partition rectangles into rows and columns.

Common Core State Standards

- **2.G.2** Partition a rectangle into rows and columns of same-size squares and count to find the total number of them.

Try It! 30 minutes | Pairs

Here is a problem about partitioning rectangles.

Maria is helping her grandmother make a blanket. She is designing a pattern for the blanket using red, blue, yellow, and green squares. The pattern is 8 rows of squares with 5 squares in each row. All the squares are the same size. How many squares are in the pattern?

Introduce the problem. Then have children do the activity to solve the problem. Distribute Color Tiles to children.

Materials
• Color Tiles (40 per pair)

1. Draw a rectangle on the board and model partitioning the rectangle into rows and columns. Explain that rows run left and right and columns run up and down. Discuss the blanket pattern with children. **Ask:** *How many squares are in each row?* Have children build the first row.

2. Have children add the second row of the pattern to form a 2 by 5 rectangle. Elicit from children that as they add additional rows they will be building larger rectangles. Elicit further that each new rectangle will still be made of equal-size squares.

⚠ Look Out!

Watch for children who count the same tiles twice or skip a tile because they are losing track of what they have counted. Suggest that they move the tiles slightly to help them keep track.

3. Ask: *How many rows are in Maria's design?* Have children finish the blanket design. **Say:** *Let's find out how many squares there are in Maria's blanket pattern. Count the squares.* **Ask:** *How many squares are needed for the blanket?*

Use Color Tiles. Build each model. Find the number of small squares in each rectangle.

(Check students' work.)

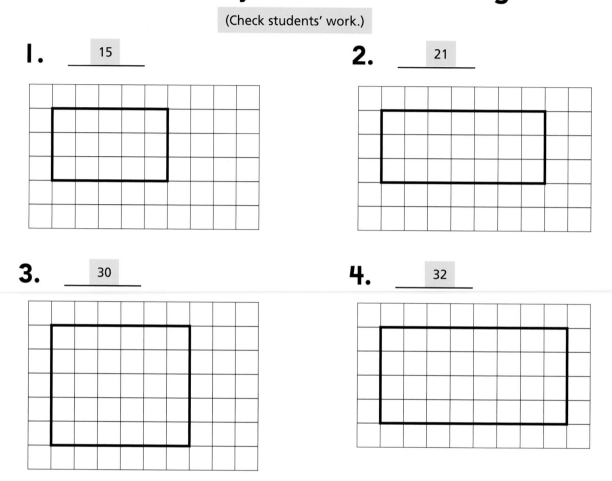

1. ___15___

2. ___21___

3. ___30___

4. ___32___

Read the story. Draw the rows and columns. Count the squares.

5. Gary is making a game board. It has 4 rows and 5 columns. It has _____ squares.

4 rows of 5 squares, 20

Download student pages at hand2mind.com/hosstudent.

© ETA hand2mind™

Answer Key

Challenge!   Mrs. Chan is making a class quilt. She has 24 children in her class. Each child will design 1 square. If she is making 6 columns on her quilt, how many rows of squares will there be? Draw the quilt to show the rows and columns of squares.

Challenge: 4 rows; Children should draw a rectangle with 4 rows of 6 squares.

_____

_____

_____

_____

_____

_____

LESSON 4

Objective

Recognize fractions as parts of a whole.

Common Core State Standards

- **2.G.3** Partition circles and rectangles into two, three, or four equal shares, describe the shares using the words *halves, thirds, half of, a third of,* etc., and describe the whole as two halves, three thirds, four fourths. Recognize that equal shares of identical wholes need not have the same shape.

Geometry

Recognizing Fractions

Introducing the basic concept of fractions to children helps them develop a foundation for deeper learning in years to come. Children need to recognize when items or sets have been divided into equal parts and to become familiar with some of the basic terminology related to simple fractions. It is important for children to understand that *equal parts* means that each person gets exactly the same amount when splitting.

Try It! *Perform the Try It! activity on the next page.*

Talk About It

Discuss the Try It! activity.

- **Ask:** *How many yellow Cuisenaire® Rods make a train that is just as long as the orange rod? What fraction of the orange rod is one yellow rod?* Guide children to understand that a yellow rod represents one-half of the orange rod.

- **Ask:** *How many red rods equal one dark green rod? What fraction of the dark green rod is one red rod?* (one-third) *How many thirds make up one dark green rod?*

- **Ask:** *How many white rods equal one purple rod? What fraction of the purple rod is one white rod?* (one-fourth) *How many fourths make up one purple rod?*

Solve It

With children, reread the problem. Then have children find how many green rods make up one blue rod. Have them draw a blue rod with three green rods below it to show their answer to the problem.

More Ideas

For other ways to teach about fractions as parts of a whole—

- Have children make Snap Cubes® trains of two, three, or four cubes. Then ask them to identify the parts that make up the whole train. For example, for a train of four cubes, ask children how many parts make up the whole. Ask them if the parts are fractions. Help them understand that one cube represents one-fourth of a four-cube train.

- Have pairs of children work with Pattern Blocks. Instruct them to select a large hexagon. Then have them see how many triangles it takes to cover the surface of the larger shape. Repeat using several combinations of large and small shapes. Discuss that the small shapes can be used to show fractions of the larger shapes.

Formative Assessment

Have children try the following problem.

Put an X under the circle that shows $\frac{1}{3}$.

A. 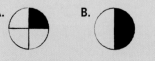 B. C.

Try It! 20 minutes | Groups of 4

Here is a problem about recognizing fractions as part of a whole.

Mario's class is using Cuisenaire Rods to learn about fractions. How can Mario find the number of light green rods that make up one blue rod?

Introduce the problem. Then have children do the activity to solve the problem. Explain that the word *fraction* means equal parts or pieces of a whole. Tell children that if a whole cake is cut into 8 equal pieces, then each piece is a fraction of the whole cake. Distribute Cuisenaire Rods, worksheets, and crayons to children.

Materials

- Cuisenaire® Rods (1 set per group)
- Rod Worksheet (BLM 17; 1 per child)
- crayons (1 crayon for every rod color per child)

1. Hold up an orange rod and explain that it represents one whole unit. Ask children to color the first rod on the Rod Worksheet to show one whole. This means that they will color the whole rod the same color. Then ask children to make a train of yellow rods that is the same length as the orange rod.

2. Explain that the small yellow rods represent fractions of the orange rod. Tell children that since two yellow rods equal one orange rod, each yellow rod is one-half of the whole. Have children color the second rod on the Rod Worksheet to show one-half of the whole.

3. Repeat using other rods to represent whole units. Have children practice finding halves, thirds, and fourths, and representing them on the Rod Worksheet. **Ask:** *How many light green rods make up a blue rod?*

⚠ Look Out!

Children may try to use a variety of colors to make equivalent trains. Remind them that fractions are equal parts of the whole, and they must use the same color to represent equal parts.

Use Cuisenaire Rods. Make each model.
Fill in the blanks. (Check students' work.)

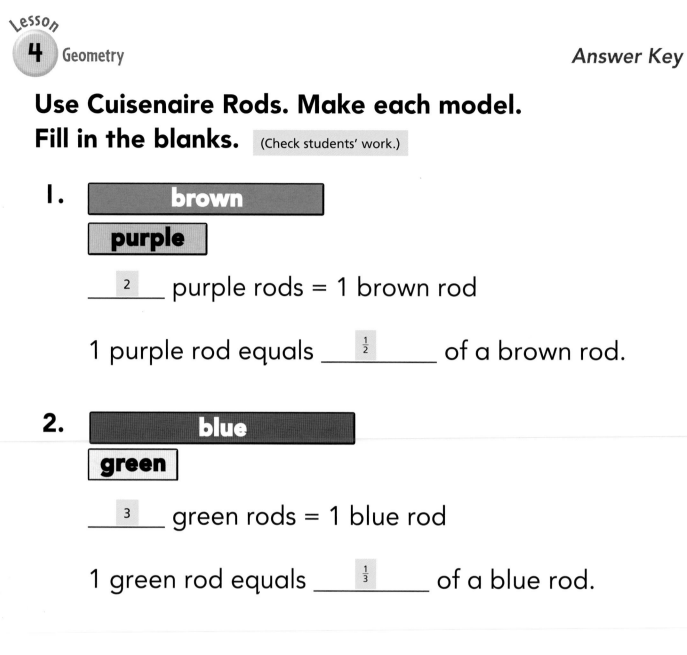

1. brown

purple

____2____ purple rods = 1 brown rod

1 purple rod equals ____$\frac{1}{2}$____ of a brown rod.

2. blue

green

____3____ green rods = 1 blue rod

1 green rod equals ____$\frac{1}{3}$____ of a blue rod.

Use Cuisenaire Rods. Use the rods named.
Draw the model. Fill in the blanks.

3. green and dark green   **4.** red and brown

1 green rod equals
____$\frac{1}{2}$____ of a dark
green rod.

1 red rod equals
____$\frac{1}{4}$____ of a
brown rod.

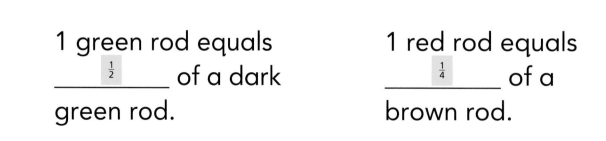 Download student pages at hand2mind.com/hosstudent.

© ETA hand2mind™

Challenge! If it takes 3 rods to equal one whole unit, what part of the whole is the smaller rod?

Challenge: $\frac{1}{3}$

_____

_____

_____

_____

_____

_____

© ETA hand2mind™

5

Objective

Identify and show halves, thirds, and fourths of regions.

Common Core State Standards

■ **2.G.3** Partition circles and rectangles into two, three, or four equal shares, describe the shares using the words *halves, thirds, half of, a third of,* etc., and describe the whole as two halves, three thirds, four fourths. Recognize that equal shares of identical wholes need not have the same shape.

Geometry

Identifying Unit Fractions

Fractions will play an important role in children's lives, and learning the basic concepts of unit fractions will give them a foundation on which they can build in the future. Being able to recognize that one-half, one-third, and one-fourth each represent equal parts of a whole will help children understand a variety of concepts, including telling time, counting money, and measurement.

Try It! Perform the Try It! activity on the next page.

Talk About It

Discuss the Try It! activity.

■ **Ask:** *How many parts were there when you first made the square?* Help children understand that the square represented one whole.

■ **Ask:** *When you added another rubber band, how many parts were there? Were the parts the same size? How could you tell?*

■ **Ask:** *What do we call two equal parts of one whole?*

■ **Ask:** *Can you divide your Geoboard into 4 equal parts that are not the same shape?*

Solve It

With children, reread the problem. Then have children draw a square to represent the gym. Have children draw a line to divide the gym in half. Extend the activity by having children draw two more squares and show what it would look like if the gym were divided into fourths and thirds. Instruct children to write one sentence about each drawing explaining which fraction is represented.

More Ideas

For other ways to teach about identifying simple fractions—

■ Have children trace different Pattern Blocks shapes and then practice dividing the tracings into halves, fourths, and thirds.

■ Have children work with a partner. Distribute Snap Cubes® to children and have them build a train. Have children trace their train four times, and divide one tracing into halves, one into fourths, and one into thirds. Have them compare the divided tracings with the undivided one so they can track the fractional division.

Formative Assessment

Have children try the following problem.

Draw lines in the squares so they match the labels.

A. halves

B. thirds

C. fourths

Try It! 20 minutes | Groups of 3

Here is a problem about identifying simple fractions.

It was raining, so Billy's class had to play in the gym for recess instead of going outside. Billy's teacher asked Billy and his friends to use a rope to divide the gym in half, one side for basketball and one side for dodgeball. How will Billy and his friends know how to place the rope?

Introduce the problem. Then have children do the activity to solve the problem.

Distribute Geoboards and rubber bands to children.

Materials
- Geoboard (1 per group)
- rubber bands (5 per group)

1. Have children make a square that is 4 units by 4 units on the Geoboard. Tell them to use another rubber band to divide the square into two equal parts. Explain that each smaller part is called a *half*.

2. Instruct children to count the units in each half of the square to verify that the parts are equal.

3. Have children divide the square into four equal parts. Explain that each part is called a *fourth*. Have children count the units in each section. To repeat with thirds, adjust the size to a 3 × 3 square or 3 × 2 rectangle.

⚠ Look Out!

Children may believe that any shape divided into two parts represents two halves, or that any shape divided into three parts represents thirds, and so on. Remind children that the parts must be equal. Reinforce this as children count the units in each section of the square during the Geoboard activity.

Use a Geoboard. Make the model shown. Into how many equals parts is the shape divided? (Check students' work.)

1.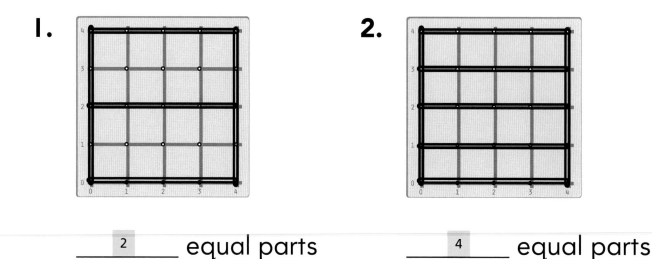

2.

_____2_____ equal parts   _____4_____ equal parts

Make a model on the grid that has equal parts. Use the number given. Draw the model. (Check students' work.)

3. 3

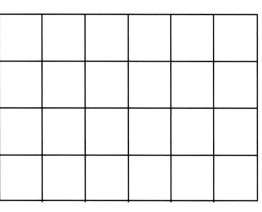

How many grid squares are in each part? __8__

4. 4

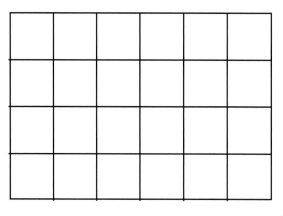

How many grid squares are in each part? __6__

© ETA hand2mind™

Challenge!   If a shape is divided into five equal parts, what part of the whole shape is each part?

Challenge: $\frac{1}{5}$

_____

_____

_____

_____

_____

_____

Name _____

Missing Numbers Worksheet

1	2	3	4	5	6	7	8	9	10
11	12	13	14	15	16	17	18	19	20
21	22	23	24	25	26	27	28	29	30
31	32	33	34	35	36	37	38	39	40
41	42	43	44	45	46	47	48	49	50
51	52	53	54	55	56	57	58	59	60
61	62	63	64	65	66	67	68	69	70
71	72	73	74	75	76	77	78	79	80
81	82	83	84	85	86	87	88	89	90
91	92	93	94	95	96	97	98	99	100

Name _____

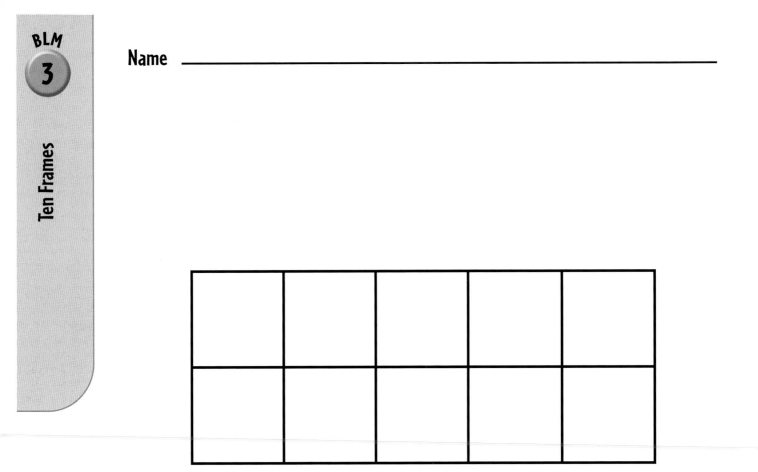

1.

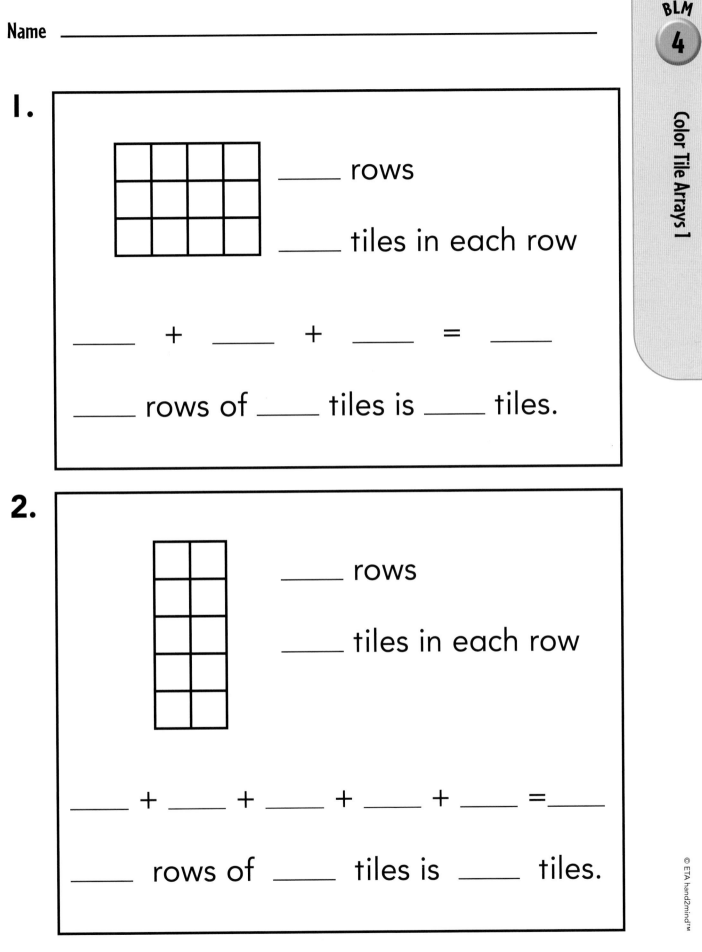

_____ rows

_____ tiles in each row

_____ + _____ + _____ = _____

_____ rows of _____ tiles is _____ tiles.

2.

_____ rows

_____ tiles in each row

____ + ___ + ___ + ___ + ___ =___

_____ rows of _____ tiles is _____ tiles.

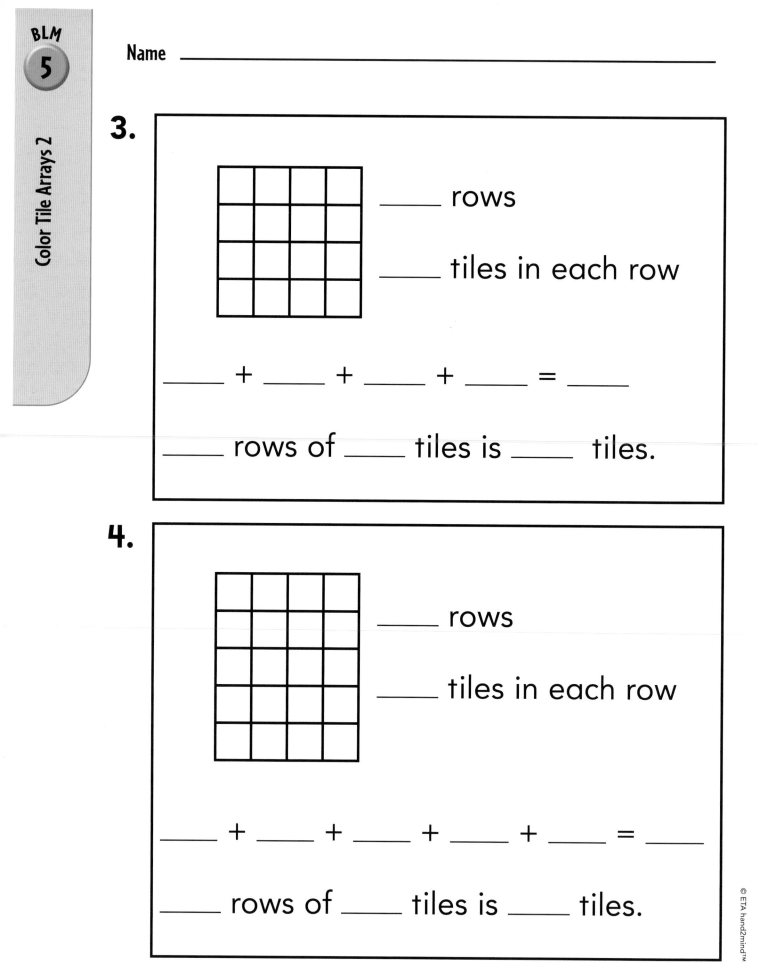

3.

_____ rows

_____ tiles in each row

_____ + _____ + _____ + _____ = _____

_____ rows of _____ tiles is _____ tiles.

4.

_____ rows

_____ tiles in each row

_____ + _____ + _____ + _____ + _____ = _____

_____ rows of _____ tiles is _____ tiles.

 Download student pages at hand2mind.com/hosstudent.

Color Tile Arrays 2

Name _____

Ones	Tens	Hundreds

Name _____

Number Forms Recording Sheet

Standard Form	Word Form
Drawing	**Expanded Form**

 Download student pages at hand2mind.com/hosstudent.

Name _____

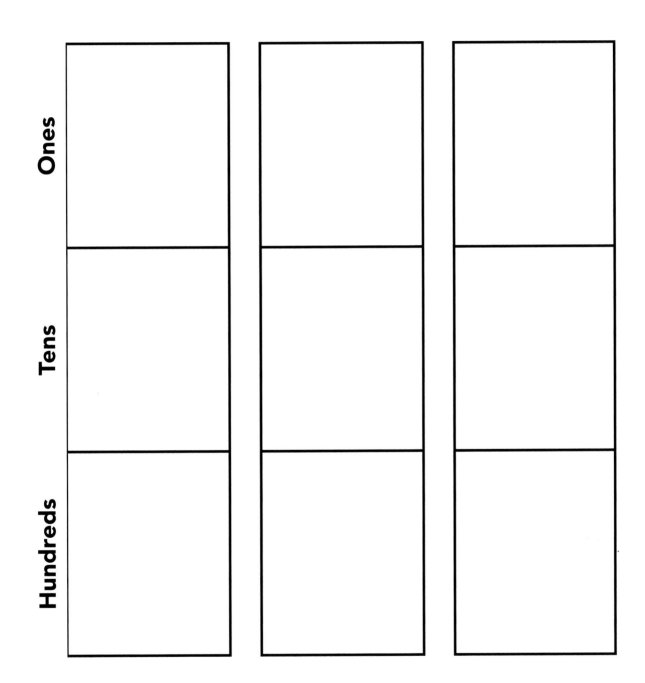

Ones	Tens	Hundreds

Name _____

Name of object: _____

It measured _____ Inchworms™ long.

It measured _____ feet long.

I should use _____ to measure this object.

Name of object: _____

It measured _____ Inchworms™ long.

It measured _____ feet long.

I should use _____ to measure this object.

Name of object: _____

It measured _____ Inchworms™ long.

It measured _____ feet long.

I should use _____ to measure this object.

Download student pages at hand2mind.com/hosstudent.

Name _____

Object	Estimate in Inches	Measurement in Inches	Estimate in Centimeters	Measurement in Centimeters

Name _____

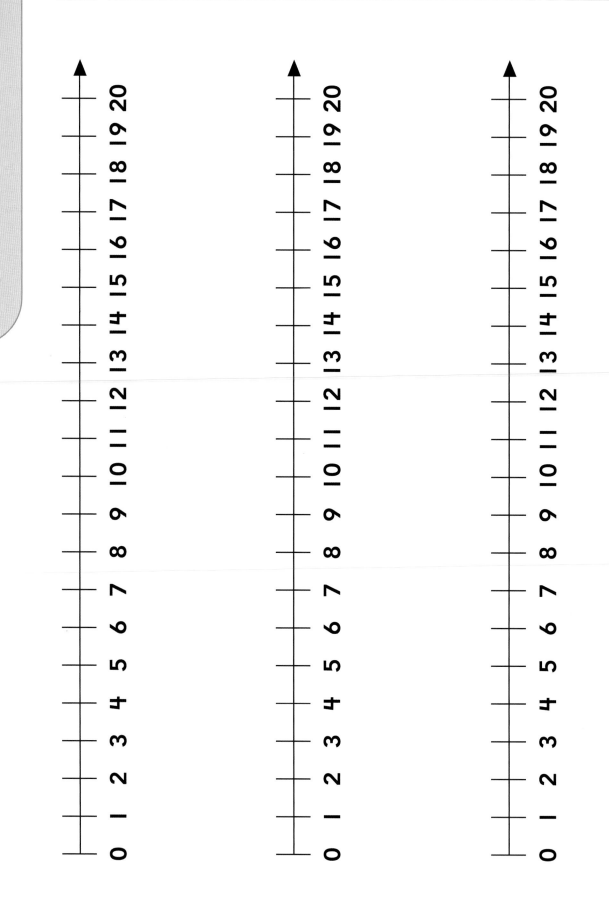

Download student pages at hand2mind.com/hosstudent.

Name _____

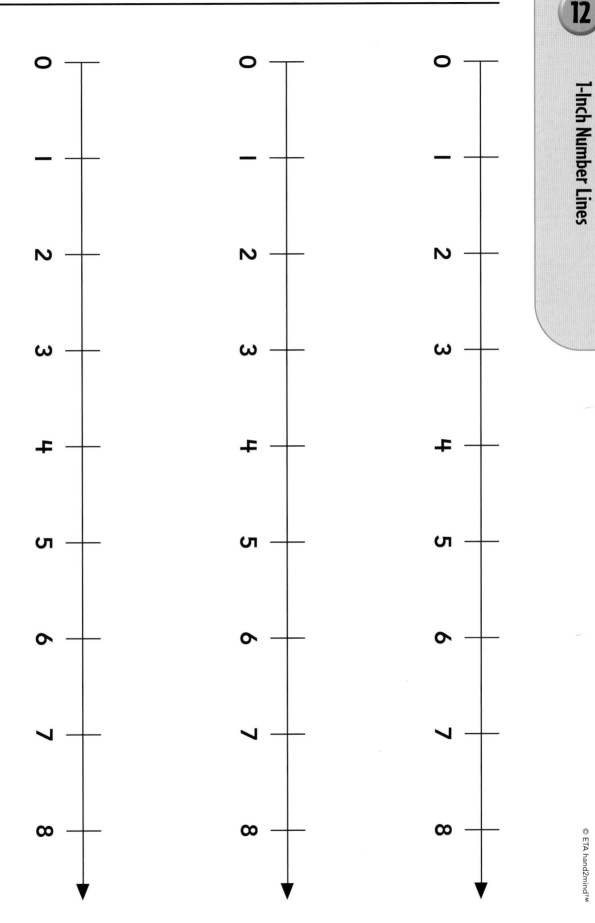

Name _____

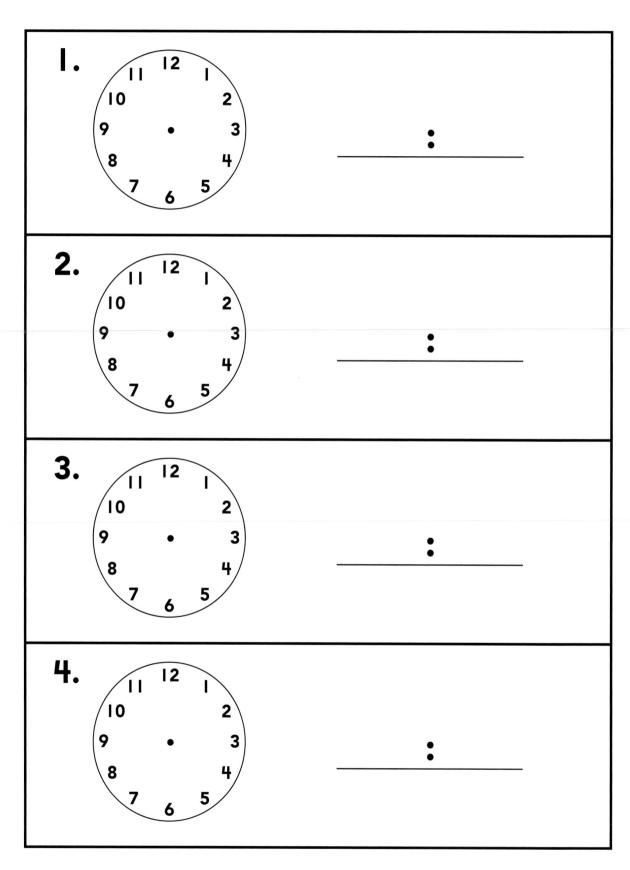

1.

2.

3.

4.

 Download student pages at hand2mind.com/hosstudent.

Name _____

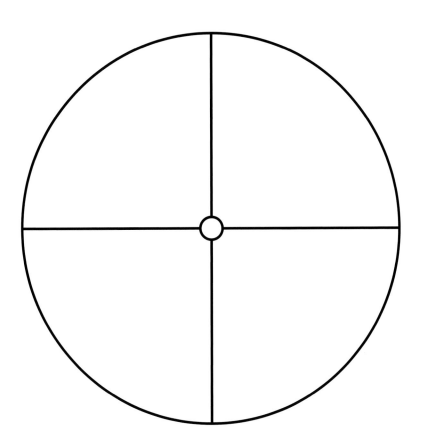

Directions: Label the spinner. Place the end of a paper clip over the center. Put the point of a pencil through the end of the paper clip. Make sure the end of the paper clip is at the center of the spinner. Spin the paper clip around the pencil. See where the paper clip stops.

Name _____

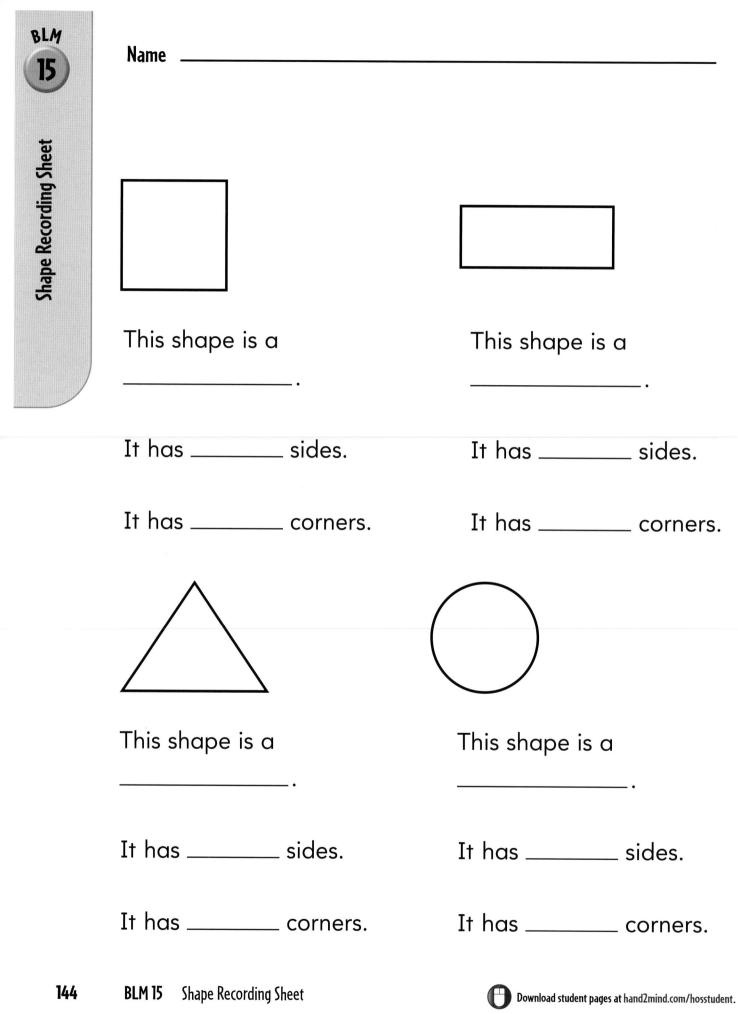

This shape is a

_____.

It has _____ sides.

It has _____ corners.

This shape is a

_____.

It has _____ sides.

It has _____ corners.

This shape is a

_____.

It has _____ sides.

It has _____ corners.

This shape is a

_____.

It has _____ sides.

It has _____ corners.

Download student pages at hand2mind.com/hosstudent.

Name of Shape	Cube	Name of Shape	Rectangular Prism
Number of Faces		Number of Faces	
Number of Edges		Number of Edges	
Number of Corners		Number of Corners	

Name

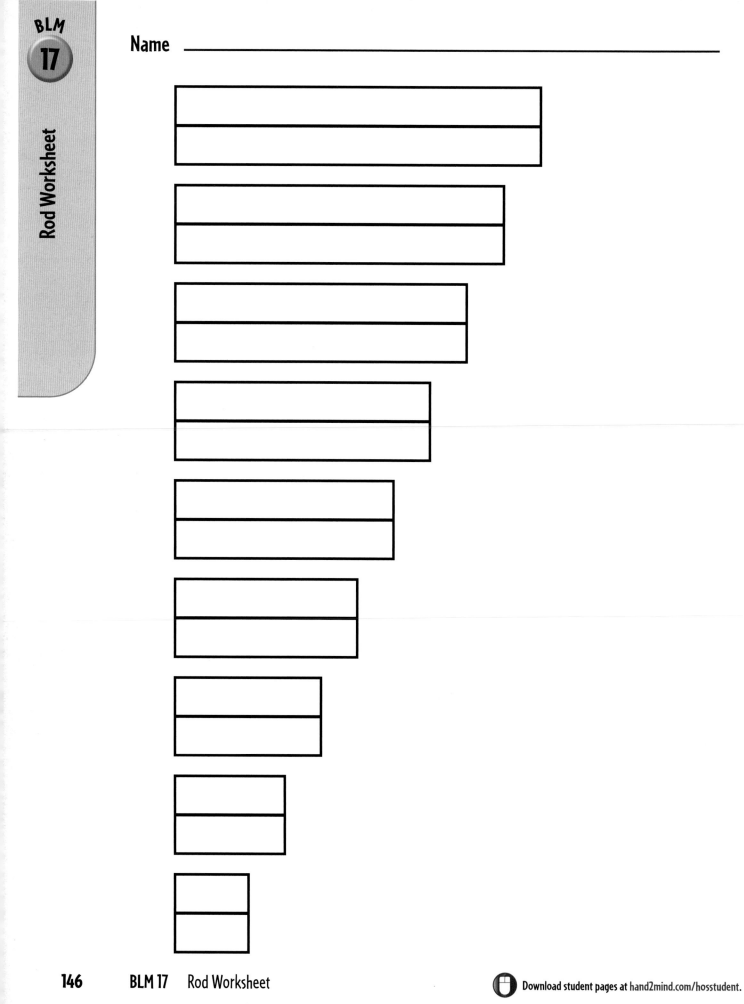

Glossary of Manipulatives

	Base Ten Blocks Base Ten Blocks include cubes representing 1,000, flats representing 100, rods representing 10, and units representing 1. The blocks can be used to teach various number and place-value concepts, such as the use of regrouping in addition and subtraction. Each unit measures 1 cm³, making the blocks ideal for measuring area and volume.
	Coin Tiles These easy-to-handle tiles help children visualize the relationships between the values of pennies, nickels, dimes, and quarters. Each tile is a hands-on area model of the coin it represents. The tiles help children see meaning in the relationships between coins and understand concepts, such as coin recognition, coin values, coin equivalence, and making change. Children can practice manipulating parts of a dollar by using the tiles with a hundred board.
	Color Tiles These 1-inch square tiles come in four different colors: red, blue, yellow, and green. They can be used to explore many mathematical concepts, including geometry, patterns, and number sense.
	Cuisenaire® Rods Cuisenaire Rods include rods of 10 different colors, each corresponding to a specific length. White rods, the shortest, are 1 cm long. Orange rods, the longest, are 10 cm long. Rods allow children to explore all fundamental math concepts, including addition and patterning, multiplication, division, fractions and decimals, and data analysis.
	Geoboard The double-sided geoboard is 7.5" square and made of plastic. One side has a 5 x 5 peg grid. The other has a circle with a 12-peg circumference. Students stretch rubber bands from peg to peg to form geometric shapes. The geoboard can be used to study symmetry, congruency, area, and perimeter.
	Geared Mini-Clock Each clock is 4" x 4" and includes a removable stand. Made of plastic, the clocks have hidden gears that reflect accurate hour and minute relationships. The hour and minute hands are color-coded to match hour and minute markings on the clock face. Clocks allow children to explore telling time on analog clocks and calculating elapsed time.
	Inchworms™ Plastic Inchworms are 1 inch long. Pieces come in six different colors and can be snapped together to make a chain. Inchworms are ideal for children who are just starting to learn measurement with standard units, as they provide a transition to using a ruler. They can be used to measure length, width, and height.

	Inchworms™ Ruler The Inchworms Ruler is made of plastic. Each inch of the ruler is marked with an Inchworm to help children see the units of measurement. The ruler can be used with compatible Inchworms to explore using standard units to measure length, width, and height.
	2-cm Color Cubes These 2-cm cubes come in six different colors. They can be used to teach counting, patterning, and spatial reasoning. They are also ideal for introducing young children to measurement of area and volume.
	Two-Color Counters These versatile counters are thicker than most other counters and easy for children to manipulate. They can be used to teach number and operations concepts, such as patterning, addition and subtraction, and multiplication and division. Counters also can be used to introduce children to basic ideas of probability.

Index

Boldface page numbers indicate when a manipulative is used in the Try It! activity.

Notes

Notes